Staying the Course

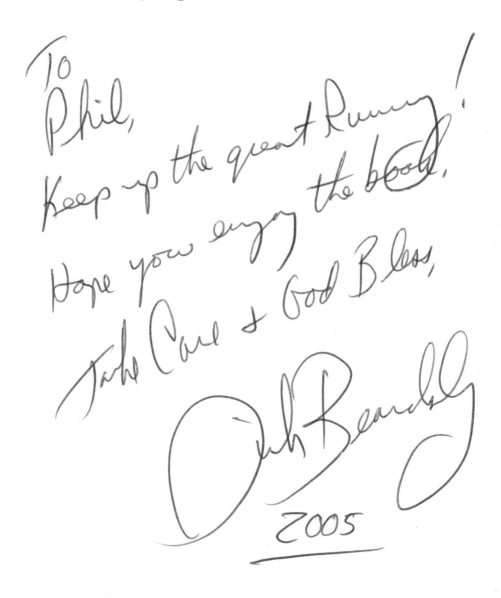

To
Phil,
Keep up the great Running!
Hope you enjoy the book.
Take Care & God Bless,

Dick Beardsley

2005

Staying the Course

A RUNNER'S
TOUGHEST
RACE

Dick Beardsley
and Maureen Anderson

University of Minnesota Press
Minneapolis / London

Published by the University of Minnesota Press
111 Third Avenue South, Suite 290
Minneapolis, MN 55401-2520
http://www.upress.umn.edu

Library of Congress Cataloging-in-Publication Data

Beardsley, Dick.
    Staying the course : a runner's toughest race / Dick Beardsley and Maureen Anderson.
        p.   cm.
    ISBN 0-8166-3759-8 (PB : alk. paper)
    1. Beardsley, Dick.   2. Runners (Sports)—United States—Biography.   I. Anderson, Maureen.   II. Title.
    GV1061.15.B44 A3 2002
    796.42'52'092—dc21

                                                                2001003716

Printed in the United States of America on acid-free paper

The University of Minnesota is an equal-opportunity educator and employer.

12 11 10 09 08 07 06 05 04   10 9 8 7 6 5 4 3 2 1

To the memory of my mom and dad,
to the memory of my godfather, Joe Ross,
and to Mary and Andy

—Dick Beardsley

To Darrell and Katie
and to my parents

—Maureen Anderson

Contents

Acknowledgments

RUNNING A MARATHON is a solitary pursuit. Writing a book
is not. It's teamwork, and we want to acknowledge the many
people who have helped us.

Thanks to Hal Higdon, senior writer for *Runner's World,*
for his encouragement and for laying the groundwork. To
Todd Orjala of the University of Minnesota Press, for his
faith in the project and for letting us say it once more: this is
a dream come true. To Adam Grafa at the Press, for his design
of the book, and to his colleagues in the production department, for sweating the small stuff. To the reference staff of
the Lake Agassiz Regional Library and the Wilson Library at
the University of Minnesota. To Tom Kelley of the New York
Road Runners. And to the world's strongest librarian, Bob
Jansen of the Minneapolis *Star Tribune.*

On a more personal note from Dick . . .

I'd like to thank my running coaches—John Fulkrod, Scott
Underwood, Bill Squires, and Bill Wenmark—without whom
there would be no story. Thanks also to Grandma's Marathon
race director Scott Keenan, for making me feel like I will always be a part of that race.

To Darold and Judy Buchta—thanks for *everything.*

To Mike, Karen, Kallie, Shana, and Ben Dunlap: who would even want to be on the course without you guys?

To Carole Ross, for taking me in.

To Mary's parents, Ed and Sylvia Hausmann. We love you.

To Sue Stenehjem-Brown, for saving my life.

To Mary and Andy, for *being* my life.

And to the good Lord, for the great story.

From Maureen . . .

Thanks to Dick, for trusting me with your story.

To Jamie Marks, Beth Walter, and Cindy Wear, for being there.

To Dick Bolles, for getting my hopes up . . . and Vince Staten, for staying in touch.

Finally, a special thanks to Darrell Anderson, whose vision, wit, and hard work are reflected on every page. You made this *fun*. We couldn't have done it without you, Sweetheart.

Dick is available for public appearances and speaking engagements. He and Maureen are both eager to hear how this book touched you. You can reach either author by e-mail at feedback@stayingthecourse.com. For more about the book, visit www.stayingthecourse.com.

Introduction

I'VE WON EVERY RACE I'VE EVER RUN.

Now, I know what you're thinking. "No he hasn't. For one thing, he lost the 1982 Boston Marathon—came in second."

And that's true. I finished two seconds behind Alberto Salazar, the world record holder at that time.

People say, "Couldn't you have found two seconds somewhere? A 26.2-mile race—couldn't you have pulled that out from somewhere?"

The answer is no.

I ran Boston as hard as I could have. The instant I crossed the finish line—and today, twenty years later—I knew there was nothing I could have done to change the outcome of that race. Nothing. I gave it everything I had.

I will never have to look back on what some people say was the most exciting race in Boston Marathon history and wonder if I could have won it had I given it more effort.

It's not that I'm happy with how everything's turned out. Even today when I read an account of the marathon or watch it on tape, I think, "Maybe if I root for myself just a little harder this time I can pull it off."

A lot of the races I've run, I didn't choose to. Like my battle with drug addiction, or my recovery from a farm accident. But in every case, I've given it my best effort and I have overcome obstacles that do a lot of people in, for good.

This book isn't about falling down and getting back up again. It's about falling down, getting run over by a car, and getting back up again. Over and over and over.

I've never wondered why I've been knocked over by tougher opponents than anyone could dream of. I know why. It's so I could pass along the secret for beating them—which is, there is no secret. It's just hard work and deep faith.

I don't know how this story turns out. I'm still working on it. But I hope you'll have fun as I catch you up on the course so far.

CHAPTER I

My Kind of Sport

I NEVER HAD DESIGNS on becoming a world-class athlete.

All I wanted was a date.

I was a junior at Wayzata High School in suburban Minneapolis when it dawned on me, the guys with the letter jackets were the ones with girlfriends. Just like that, I decided to go out for football. I found the coach to tell him the news.

"Hey Coach! I'm going out for football!"

"Good, Beards! We need a water boy!"

"No, I'm serious," I told him. "I want to play football."

He looked at me. I'm six feet tall and weighed 130 back then. He shrugged. I wasn't discouraged.

I showed up for the first practice, fired up. Once I figured out how to get all the equipment on, that is. I would do things in the wrong order and have to start over. Everyone else had been on the field for a while by the time I got there.

Coach decided to get it over with. "Beardsley! Fumble!" he hollered, just to see what I'd do. Twenty guys were standing around and watching, but it didn't faze me. I dove on the ball. I heard a bunch of cracks and thought, what happened? I couldn't breathe! All twenty guys were on top of me, the first tackle of the first practice of the season.

They got up, I got up, my helmet was on crooked, and my head felt like it would explode.

"That's it," I decided. "I'm going to be a bachelor the rest of my life." It didn't bother me a bit. I couldn't get back to the locker room fast enough to get out of that crap.

"You ought to come out for cross-country," my friend George Ross said a few days later.

"Cross-country? What's that?"

"Aw Dick, it's fun, man," he told me. "We run through the woods and the swamps and the fields. You just run."

That's my kind of sport, I thought. I was already doing that, hiking in the woods all the time.

"We're having practice tomorrow morning," he said. "Eight o'clock."

"I'll be there!" I told him.

The next morning I was the first to pull into the parking lot. I sat there in my rusted old Datsun pickup, waiting for the others. I had my running gear on, or what I thought was close enough.

The guys pulled up and got out of their vehicles. They had shiny sweats and multicolored shoes on, and . . . I couldn't face them. I dove for the floor of my truck, but it was no use. They knew I was in it. A couple guys pulled me out, everybody took one look at me and oh, I've never heard anyone laugh that hard in my *life*.

I hadn't been able to find my white gym shorts that morning, which would've been bad enough. All that was left was a pair of white shorts that belonged to my dad. He weighed about two hundred pounds, though, so I had a black belt holding them up. You get a good wind and drop me out of an airplane, I'd have looked like Mary Poppins floating down to earth.

Mary Poppins, in blue bumper tennis shoes and a pair of my dad's black socks that went up to my knees.

I tried to remember what was so bad about football.

Somehow—it took forever—the laughter subsided long enough for Coach to get a word in: "Okay guys, we're going to run around the block today." Run around the block! This'll be great, I thought. I looked at George. He was up in front, looking like the stud he was—a state champion in the indoor mile. Coach blew the whistle and off we went.

I was fired up again. We were all in a big pack, running. We got up to the first corner and took a left. We got up to the next block and took another left. One more block, I thought, and we'll be heading back to the school. But the guys kept going straight. "They must be feeling good today," I thought. "They're going to go two blocks." We got to the next block and I got ready to take a left, but they kept going straight. By then I was having trouble keeping up. Good thing. I didn't want them to hear how hard I was breathing.

Every chance there was to take a left, the guys just kept going straight. We were out of town by then, north of it, out in the country. I couldn't see anyone. They were gone. I thought they might be running out to the Hennepin County Workhouse and back. That's about three miles. I decided "around the block" must be cross-country lingo for a three-mile run.

That was fine with me. It was a really pretty route. You go by Parker's Lake and all the farm buildings. But it was getting harder to keep running, and I had to slow down. I walked much of the rest of the way in, about a mile.

I got back to school and everyone was gone. The parking lot was empty. Everyone had already taken showers and gone home.

Me, I was exhausted—but strangely happy. That feeling! I'd just run three miles and no one had tackled me. I couldn't get that out of my mind.

Until then, the most I'd ever run was from one end of the basketball court to the other. Something went off in my brain. I felt calm, and happy.

This was going to be my sport.

I got home and had trouble containing myself. "Mom!" I hollered, bursting through the door. "I'm going to be on the cross-country team!" I told her all about it. She couldn't shut me up. Next thing I knew, we were headed out the door to go shopping. It didn't take me long to find them, a pair of red leather Adidas running shoes. The next day I got my uniform, a blue T-shirt with "Wayzata Cross Country" in gold letters, and bright blue shorts with a gold stripe.

I put the uniform on and I was a different person. My shoulders straightened, I had a little more confidence. I'd always had plenty of friends, from 4-H and other activities, but there was something about being in sports. I felt like I was really one of the guys.

We practiced every night after school. We met about three-thirty and went until five. As I got into it a little more, I thought we could have the top touch football team in the state of Minnesota. Nothing against Coach, he was the nicest guy you'd ever want to meet. But a typical practice for him was, "Okay guys, go out and run four miles. Then come back and we'll have a game of touch football." That was our workout. He used touch football as a reward, which it probably would have been for him. I never got the feeling he was that into running. He was always off to the side, smoking.

Me, I went from excited to obsessed in about a week. Coach would say, "Okay guys, go out and run the downtown Wayzata route," and half the guys would cut corners and take shortcuts. "Why would you want to do that?" I wondered. I always took the long route. I knew the only way I was going to get better was by working at this, and I wanted a letter jacket.

That was my goal. A letter jacket, and the dates I was sure would follow.

All you had to do to earn a letter jacket was be in one varsity meet. In varsity you could run seven runners, and your first five counted in the scoring. But all seven qualified for a letter jacket.

I was on the JV team, but the JV and varsity runners were always in the same meets. Usually the meets were on Mondays. They started right away in September, so we didn't have a lot of practice leading up to the first one. The first couple of meets I finished in the middle of the pack for our JV, but I quickly improved. Within three weeks I was usually the number one runner on the JV team.

We all rode the same bus to the meets. I was usually half asleep on the way, having gotten up early to milk cows or do other farm chores for neighbors. One of the last meets of the season Coach was rattling off the varsity roster and all of a sudden I heard "Beardsley." I woke up. I was the seventh runner on varsity!

I got in the race—it was three miles, as usual—and I went out like a crazed person. I was at or near the front of the pack for much of the race just from the excitement. Eventually I faded, but I finished our fifth runner. I counted in the scoring! You'd have thought I'd won the Olympic gold medal. I felt like I could clear the pole vault bar without benefit of the pole. I was getting a letter jacket and I counted in the scoring! I didn't even recognize myself, that's how much better I suddenly felt about life.

Not only did I ask a girl out to homecoming, I asked one of the cheerleaders. And she said yes! Up to that point I was one of those guys who'd call a girl on the phone and hang up in a panic the minute she answered. Not anymore. Things were going to be different.

When cross-country season ended, I kept running. I loved it. George and I were becoming best friends and we ran together. Evenings, weekends, we probably ran more days than not. His dad, Joe, ran with us too, timing us. I'd gotten to know Joe during the season, and took to him right away. He was at every meet, cheering us on and hollering encouragement.

It got to where I practically lived with George. We usually ran at his place. They lived even farther out in the country than we did, and there were some great trails back in the woods. Sometimes we ran on the gravel roads near his place, or on trails they had in their pasture.

On weekends we had our donut run, when Joe and his wife, Carole, invited all the kids over from the cross-country team. We'd go for a long run, then come back to piles of homemade donuts. It was great. I started to feel as much a part of the Ross family as I did my own, maybe more.

Joe Ross was the biggest fan of running I'd ever met, or ever would meet. He got me hooked. Because of him, I associated running with fun—and that's the key to everything. It's such a gift. If you're going to be a good runner, you have to put the miles in, and he was always there for me. If the wind was blowing thirty miles an hour on a January afternoon when it was twenty below, Joe drove me out ten or fifteen miles and dropped me off so I could run with the wind at my back.

Joe Ross was also the father figure I sorely needed. My dad sold women's clothing to stores in five states and for nine months of the year he was hardly ever home. It seemed like all he did when he *was* home was drink and fight with my mom.

George was big into track, too, but I barely knew what that was. The spring of my junior year the coaches were thinking, this Beardsley, he's turning into a good runner, he could be one of our top guys. "So Beards, you coming out for track?" one of them finally asked. "Track?" I said. "Is that where you run around a bunch of times in a circle? No way. That's fishing season."

Even today, there isn't a whole lot that comes between me and fishing. Dad wasn't around a lot during the school year, but he had much of the summers off, and we spent that time together on his boat. "Do you want to go fishing?" he'd say. He might as well have asked a dog if he wanted to play fetch. I couldn't climb into the car fast enough. Fishing was so much a part of my life from the very beginning, sometimes I wonder if when I was born my dad didn't just scoop me up in the hospital blanket and tell my mom, "Thanks for having a boy. See ya, we're going fishing."

It took the coaches a while to forgive me for not going out for track, but that hardly registered. I had my letter jacket and I was looking forward to cross-country again, but track did not appeal to me at all.

That is, until a running camp I attended that summer at the University of Wisconsin at River Falls. It was there I learned how important track work is if you want to run distances. I decided to go out for track my senior year.

By the summer George and I were practically inseparable. He'd graduated and was going to Mankato State on an athletic scholarship. We ran together every day, usually in the evenings since I was a fishing guide and had farm work to do during the day. Evenings were a better time to run anyway since it was cooler.

We'd do a run through the countryside, starting at George's place, on the gravel roads. We took the back roads up through this little town of Hamel, about five miles north of Wayzata. After that we'd head back toward their place. Joe was almost always out there with us, timing us and keeping us motivated.

We got into some pretty good battles. On an eight- or ten-mile run, we didn't say boo to each other for about the last five because we were trying to drive each other into the ground. The minute we'd finish we were best friends again, but those last five miles we tried to bury each other. Coming down the final half-mile stretch—they lived on a gravel road and as you got closer to their house it was a gradual downhill—we just flew. We flew down that hill. Joe was out there with his stopwatch, waiting at the finish where he could put his arms around us both and tell us how great we did. Most of the time George edged me out at the very end because he had a really good kick, but there were many times we finished right together.

When I started running, I didn't realize it was going to be my life. All I knew was how much I loved it. From the first time I felt better about myself, I had more confidence, and it was addictive.

I ran a lot of miles that summer before my senior year, and when the cross-country season began I was co-captain of the team. I soon became our top runner. That's not saying a whole lot because I never got to a state or even a regional meet. But I was improving steadily and was probably at least as dedicated as anyone on the team.

I was the number one runner for every cross-country meet my senior year. Every meet we ran three miles. That was back before they made it a 5K race, 3.1 miles. Every race I took off like a crazed person. That was the only way I knew how to run. I ran as fast as I could for as long as I could. I'd get out in front, and have a twenty-, thirty-, forty-yard lead on the others. I found out the coaches at the other schools told their kids, "You know Beardsley's going to go out hard, you know he's going to fade, so don't worry about him." And that's exactly what happened.

I'd get out there in the lead, but about halfway through the race, the pack would start catching up with me. I'd hang with them for a while, but with about a half mile to go I'd be spent. Once in a while I'd win a meet, but against the better schools I'd usually finish fifth or sixth, something like that.

I continued to spend most of my free time at George's house, even though he was away at school. It was so much fun over there. I ate at their place almost every meal. Joe continued to encourage my running. "You know, Dick," he'd say, "you're a good runner. Always believe that." He was still out there with me all the time. We'd go into his pasture and he'd time me, running between the cow pies. He already had the brush cleared away and the trails widened a little bit. He had this quarter-mile lap set up in the woods, so I could run repeat quarters—each a little faster than the one before. His voice was soothing, even though he was yelling. He kept a close eye on his stopwatch and never let up on the encouragement. He stood at the ready, with juice or water. He made me feel like I was important, and I worshiped him.

It never seemed to bother my parents that I was never at home, that I was always at the Rosses'. Things continued to get worse between Mom and Dad. They were caught up in their own problems. I tried to ignore the drinking and fighting. I'd just take my dog, Sam, and go for a hike in the woods. I was in choir, I played basketball, I fished and trapped and did farm chores and hung out with my buddies. I told myself I was having a very happy childhood. My sister, Mary Ann, made a point of telling me I wasn't. "You always run away from what's happening at home;" she'd say. Who could blame me?

Joe continued to come to all of my meets, even though George was away at college. By then our school had girls' cross-country, and a couple of the Ross girls were on the team. But Joe would have come to the meets even if they weren't. He made it clear, I was family.

I had one goal my senior year in cross-country and that was to break sixteen minutes for three miles. Obviously if you come in at fifteen minutes flat, you're running five-minute miles. I just wanted to come in at fifteen-something. I didn't care if it was 15:59.9.

It was one of the last meets of the season, and Joe kept telling me I could do it. I was so determined to break sixteen minutes I felt like I was possessed. I ran as hard as I ever had, and with about a quarter mile to go Joe hollered, "Dick! You're going to do it! You're going to break sixteen minutes!" I was dying, but digging down the best I could. I came across the finish line, the official yelled "16:01!"—and I said it. The F word. I'd never said the F word to myself. I'd never even *thought* the F word. And now there it was, the F word, suspended in midair where all the officials and coaches and teachers and parents could take it in.

I wasn't even out of the chute before I turned around to say, "Oh, I am *so sorry* for what I just said!" I took a deep breath and fought tears, I was that upset and embarrassed. "That is *not me,*" I continued. "I just wanted to break sixteen minutes and got caught up in the emotion."

The public apology taken care of, I approached every single coach and parent who was there and told them how sorry I was. I could've been disqualified from the race, but that was the last thing on my mind. I was really, truly sorry for what had happened.

Decades later it still bothers me.

Swear words were not in my vocabulary, but I had a way of bringing them out in others. My running coach at the University of Minnesota-Waseca, Dr. John Fulkrod, probably credits every gray hair on his head to the years we spent together.

One Friday evening in the spring of my final year at Waseca, we were chalking the track together and getting ready for our home invitational meet the next day. It was the biggest event of the season. The stands would be filled with people from all over the community as well as our junior college. Coach was looking forward to a great showing. Everybody was excited.

The phone rang at the concession stand. *"Beardsley!!"* Coach hollered a minute later. "Get *over* here!" He was screaming his head off and I thought, whatever it is, I'm in deep trouble. He couldn't even look at me, he was that furious. "When you were in Detroit for that indoor meet," he asked, "did you miss some tests?" Well, yeah. "Well why in *hell* weren't they made up?" I don't know, I told him. I just never got around to it. "You're ineligible," he said, getting more to the point. "You can't run tomorrow." I froze. What then? I had no idea what to do. A few seconds went by, but it felt like ten minutes. I started walking back to where I was chalking. "Oh no you don't," he snapped. "I don't want you around. Just get out of here."

I ran back to the school, a couple miles from the track, and had time to think about how I had let Coach down. Plenty of time to scheme. I had to find the dairy science professor and see if he'd give me another test before tomorrow morning. How I would talk him into that, I didn't know. But Jim would. Jim was a high jumper and a good buddy of mine. He was great at pulling off the impossible.

Jim reminded me the professor, John, had a reputation for having plenty of girlfriends. He was probably in the Cities visiting one of them. "We have to find his black book," Jim said. Which of course was probably locked in his office.

Lucky for us, I was in good with the janitors at school. We talked one of them into letting us into John's office. Jim started going through his desk drawers and found the black book. He started calling girlfriends one by one. By then it was going on eight o'clock, and we were running out of names. Suddenly one said, "Yeah, he's here." Jim talked to him. Fortunately he was a big-time track fan and took pity on me. I got on the phone. "Dick, here's the deal," he said. "I'll drive back to Waseca early tomorrow morning. You meet me in my office at eight o'clock, and I'll give you an oral exam. All I can say is, you'd better study for it."

He didn't ask how we found him, and we didn't volunteer it.

Of course I hadn't opened a book in this class. We found another buddy who was really smart, and he and I and a couple other guys stayed up all night together. The three of them quizzed me while we downed diet colas and tried to stay awake.

I got to John's office at eight o'clock sharp and was just wiped. He started. It took about forty-five minutes. He checked it and said, "You got an eighty-five. You're eligible." He called the track. Coach was already there getting things set up. "Dick came in this morning and took the test," he said. "He's eligible."

I got to the track and was pumped in a way I'd never been pumped before, though much of that was being punchy from no sleep. I was wired, and determined to make this up to Coach. That was all that mattered. He still wasn't in the mood to talk to me, though. "I'm glad you got your shit together," was all he offered.

I was supposed to run the six-mile and the steeplechase that morning as warm-ups for the mile and the three-mile. Coach wanted me to take the first two events real easy and just use them to get ready for the events he needed me for the most.

The gun went off in the six-mile and I flew. I won the race easily. "Beardsley!" Coach hollered. "You're supposed to be taking these easy!" "I *am,* Coach!" I hollered back. "I feel great!"

Twenty minutes later it was time for the steeplechase, which is about a two-mile run where you jump over barriers. "You'd better sit out of the steeplechase," Coach said. "I didn't expect you to run that hard." "No way," I told him. "Put me in it. I'm running."

I won the steeplechase. Coach looked at my time and it was about 9:40. "Well, that's it for the day," he said. "You're done." "Aw Coach," I told him, "I just want to try the mile. Put me in it."

By then I'd had a little bit of a break and felt terrific. The gun went off in the mile and a guy from Rochester Junior College was giving me a race. We were flying. It was him and me. With a lap to go, everyone else was way behind us. Coming around the last corner we were dead even, but I outleaned him at the line and I won. I won the mile.

"That is clearly enough for today," Coach said, abandoning any plans to put me in the three-mile. "Coach, let me in there," I pleaded. "I just want to pace Dean." By then he knew better than to argue.

I won the three.

All the distance races they had that day, I won every one. On no sleep.

"You are the only guy who can take Coach from furious to ecstatic in two hours," my good friend and teammate Bob Frandsen pointed out.

It wasn't the first time.

In my second year of cross-country at Waseca I qualified for the national championships in Long Island, as did Owen Dickey, my roommate. Coach Fulkrod and his wife, Linda, accompanied the two of us to New York City. Owen and I were just a couple of country bumpkins from Minnesota. We flew into JFK airport, saw all those buildings, and just freaked. We got there late on a Thursday and the meet was on Saturday. Coach had meetings Friday and didn't object when Owen and I wanted to take the rental car to do a little sightseeing.

Sightseeing in downtown Manhattan, though naturally we didn't tell Coach that.

I was at the wheel. Owen was in the front seat with me, trying to make sense of the map. We got into the city and drove by the Empire State Building, our tongues on the floor of the car we were so awe inspired, and we tried to find a place to park. It took forever, but I finally pulled down a road with plenty of parking spaces—but no cars. There weren't any signs that said no parking. "Owen!" I said. "This is great!" We were right off Fifth Avenue.

The rest of the day, we were like two hamsters in a wheel factory. We raced from landmark to landmark—the Empire State Building, the World Trade Center, everything. It was November and the days were short. Before we knew it the sun was down. "We need to get some things to take home to people," Owen said, so we did the round of souvenir shops and in no time it was going on seven o'clock.

We headed back toward the rental car. We walked down

the street where it was parked and saw flashing lights. A tow truck drove by. "Gee, that kind of looks like our car, doesn't it?" I mentioned to Owen. Then I saw a present in the back window, one we'd found earlier. "Owen!" I screamed. "That's our car!"

Luckily right then the truck driver hit a stop light and we took off after him. "Sir," I said, trying to get my breath back. "This is our car. Could you just pull over and unhook it so we can get back?" He looked like he was Puerto Rican, and for a split second I wondered if he could speak English. He just stared at me. It must've dawned on him what he was dealing with. "I'd love to," he said, "but I've already called it in. I have to take it to the impound lot." He paused. "Tell you what," he said, taking pity on us. "Hop in, and you can ride there with me."

We got there, and I started talking to a cop—or at least he looked like a cop. "I don't get it," I told him, as respectfully as I could considering the panic I felt. "There weren't any no parking signs around." "There were signs all over the place," he said, like he wasn't interested in pursuing the subject. "If you want your car it's going to cost you a hundred bucks." A hundred bucks! Owen dug into his pocket, and I dug into mine. Between the two of us we had $101. I hoped we didn't have to buy gas.

Then I realized, running out of gas in the worst area of New York City would be a kinder fate than what awaited us at the hotel. It was going on ten when we got back, we'd been gone all day, and I thought, oh my God, they probably sent the posse out looking for us. It took every ounce of courage we had to knock on the door of the room where the coaches were meeting.

"Where the *hell* have you been?" Coach wanted to know, looking not the slightest bit relieved that we were okay. Oh did we get reamed. We were crying and he didn't care. He wanted an explanation and he wanted it now. If I hadn't known him better, I'd have thought he was putting on a show for the other coaches, he was chewing our butts that bad. "Get to your rooms," he finally said. "You guys had better run well tomorrow."

We slunk out of the room, ashamed. The door closed behind us. There was no one in the hallway and it was eerie it was so quiet. We got about ten feet down the hall and all of a sudden the room where the coaches were just *erupted* in laughter. Maybe they thought we ran to the elevator, because it was clear they had no idea we could hear every word. "Can you believe it?" one said. "Can't you just imagine the look on their faces when they saw their car being towed?" It sounded like a couple of them might start choking, they were laughing so hard.

Owen and I didn't lose any sleep over it after that.

The next morning I ran the best race of my life, finishing the five-mile course in 24:50. It was the first time I'd run five miles at a sub five-minute pace. Not enough to win, but a big milestone for me.

I was starting to deliver on the potential Coach Fulkrod saw in me from the start. I'd only known him about two weeks when one night after practice—I was always the last to leave—he put his arm around me and said, "Dick, I think you can become as good a runner as you want to be." I never forgot that. As hard as I'd been working, it made me want to work even harder.

It was in junior college that I started putting in the occasional hundred-mile week. I'd get up and go for a run in the morning, about seven o'clock—usually five miles. Then we had our regular afternoon workout, usually eight or ten miles at least. That might consist of track runs, it might be a long run, it might be fartlek. Fartlek is where you race toward something, then back off a little bit, then race toward something else, then back off. Over and over.

Regardless of the workout, it was rare I didn't put in thirteen or fourteen miles a day—even on weekends.

The thing that was great about being at a junior college

was, I would have been lost at the main university. Not just academically—I was barely hanging on as it was. But at a bigger school I probably wouldn't even have come close to making the junior varsity team. I was so thrilled to have a coach, especially one I liked this well, and I lived to make him proud of me. If he said, okay guys, go do ten miles, it wasn't 9.9. It was at least 10.2.

The only time I blew him off was when he suggested I take a day off once in a while. It was against my religion. I couldn't do it. Until I was forced to, that is. The winter following my second cross-country season I slipped on some ice and tore cartilage in my knee, which required surgery and was the first of several injuries that have plagued me ever since. I didn't know that, of course. The only thing I thought was in jeopardy was the spring track season.

Coach and I hatched a plan. We decided I'd sit out spring track that year and be his first redshirt. I'd probably need more credits beyond summer school to graduate anyway. Why not come back for a third full year? Money, for one thing, but Coach had a way around that, too. Coincidentally there were some things going on with him that a break from coaching cross-country would help with. I couldn't be on the team since I'd used up my eligibility, but I could coach. The money would help me eke by another year. I'd coach cross-country in the fall and be on the track team the following spring.

I didn't admit it, but the break from running to let my knee heal was good for me, mentally and physically. More and more I'd been thinking about the junior college championships. "You know, Dick," Coach would say, "you could run the marathon in junior college." Until then I'd never really thought about a marathon. The longest I'd ever run in training was about fourteen miles. The marathon intrigued me. I'd matured a lot since high school, and had won a fair number of cross-country meets. The strange thing was, it seemed like the farther I got in a race, the stronger I got. When most people started to fade, I got faster and faster.

I didn't know why. Maybe because the longer races were more fun. You hit a bad spot in a mile and it's over with. In a longer race, you can hit a bad spot, recover, and still get back into it.

My strong suit was holding a pace. I could run at a five-minute pace, take it down to 4:40, recover at five-minute, then take it back down to 4:40 for however long I needed to. I tried to punish people by surging a lot as a race progressed to where I didn't have to rely on a good kick at the end. The goal was to make them hurt so much they were just hanging on, so that as we finished I'd have more left than they did.

A long race was like a chess game to me: fun.

I ran my first marathon on a whim, the Paavo Nurmi race in Hurley, Wisconsin. Paavo Nurmi was a great Finnish runner and there are a lot of Finnish people in that area. I didn't tell anyone about the race. I just drove up there myself and rented a room in a little ten-dollar-a-night motel.

The race was August 13, 1977.

I hadn't trained for a marathon. This was just an experiment. I got in the race and was running along, feeling great, mile after mile. I got to running with this guy, and was yakking away. After a little while he said, "Hey Dick, I don't mean to be rude, but man, I'm not talking to you anymore. You'll find out. The marathon takes a lot out of you."

I didn't believe him, necessarily, at least not at the twelve-, thirteen-mile point. It just didn't seem like that big of a deal. At fifteen, sixteen miles it didn't seem so either. But at about eighteen miles it was pretty tough going. I finished the marathon, though, with a time of 2:47:14, placing sixtieth. I thought, well, that was interesting.

Two months later I was out for my morning run and bought the Minneapolis paper on the way back to my dorm room, as usual. There was an item in the sports section about the City of Lakes Marathon—that's the one they had before the Twin Cities Marathon came along. This one started at the southeast corner of Lake Calhoun and went four and a half times around Calhoun and Harriet, just big loops around two lakes right in the middle of Minneapolis.

It was Tuesday and the race was Sunday.

I thought, well, I only have five days—I wonder if there's anything I can do to get ready. I was coaching cross-country that season, so Coach Fulkrod wasn't around to tell me how crazy I was. I still had never trained for a marathon. Paavo Nurmi hadn't been so much fun that I'd suddenly decided to become a marathoner.

Okay, I thought, what can I do in five days? I skipped my first class that morning—not what you'd call a big sacrifice—and pulled out my boxes of running magazines. There had to be something on marathons. Sure enough. It wasn't just an article about training for a marathon, it was about how to train for an ultra marathon—fifty miles. These people were talking about how they could run fifty miles and float like a butterfly the entire time, they felt that good. It sounded great.

All you had to do was fast for a week.

I don't have a week, I thought, but I have five days. I'd already had breakfast, but decided that would be it. I was allowed to drink water, Gatorade, and juice. I drank plenty of all three to stave off the worst of the hunger pangs. By Saturday morning my stomach felt really weird, so I had a chocolate milk shake. I told myself that because I could drink it, it wasn't food.

Saturday night I stayed with my dad. I didn't tell him why I was in town. He was going to the Vikings game the next day and wouldn't be around anyway.

Race day was perfect. Cool and crisp, with no wind. I was so new to marathoning it didn't occur to me how stupid my next move was: a little warm-up run around the two lakes and through a few neighborhoods. Seven or eight miles!

I got to the starting line and thought, I have to find someone who knows what they're doing. I saw Barney Klecker and some others. They were good runners. What the heck. I'd just run with them.

The gun went off and we went through the first mile in about five minutes, five seconds. I could barely do that in a five-mile race, and here I was doing it in a marathon. The first thing that occurred to me was how good I felt. The next thing I decided was it must be the fasting.

We got to three miles and there was an aid station. All of a sudden Barney and company made their way over for water. Those stupid fools, I thought, everybody knows you don't want to drink during a marathon because you'll get a side ache. Well, of course it's just the opposite, but I didn't know that. I didn't drink the entire race.

At three miles I felt great. Four miles, five miles, six miles went by—same thing.

My goal was to finish in the top ten. If you were one of the top ten runners you got a little trophy. It wasn't such a great trophy or anything. It almost looked like a bowling trophy with the bowling ball broken off, but I wanted it desperately.

I felt really good. I was running in the lead pack and it was great. All of a sudden at about eight or nine miles my feet started aching. I didn't understand. I'd never had any problems with blisters. I looked down and my new blue shoes were now a really pretty purple. My feet were like hamburger, they were bleeding that much.

Oh.

The day before I'd gone to a running store and tried on a pair of Nike waffle trainers, at least that's what they called them at the time. I put them on, walked about twenty feet, and told the guy I'd take them. I reached for my billfold with one hand and used the other hand to put them back in the box. "Don't you want to wear them out of the store to break them in a little bit?" the guy wanted to know. "Nah," I said.

"I'm running in a marathon tomorrow morning. I don't want to get them dirty."

After about another mile, my feet went numb, and that was the end of my problems with them.

We were about halfway at that point. Barney and a couple other guys were still in front and starting to pull away a little bit. I was in fourth or fifth place and felt like I could hang onto it. I was going along, got to about fifteen miles and thought, I feel really good. This wall you supposedly hit at twenty miles, I didn't see that happening to me.

Sure enough, at twenty miles, I felt pretty darned good.

I got to twenty-one miles, and was still in fourth or fifth place.

Twenty-two miles, same thing.

At twenty-three miles, I wasn't exactly daisy fresh—but felt pretty good, considering.

At twenty-three miles and a step and a half, it was over. It felt like an elephant had jumped out of a tree onto my shoulders and was making me carry it the rest of the way in. Everything hurt so badly I started crying. Every step I took was another step straight through hell. I couldn't even keep my eyes open because I was hallucinating.

A good friend of mine from high school had been watching the race. He came up alongside me and wanted to know if it would help if he ran beside me a while. He knew I was hurting. "Thanks," I mumbled. Up until then I'd been in the top ten runners, but suddenly all these people were just flying by me. "Trip them!" I told Chris and I meant it. "Throw them in the lake, tackle them, do what you have to do. I have to finish in the top ten."

"You're lapping people," he told me. "They still have to go around another loop after this."

If I hadn't been dying, I would have felt good about that, but all I could think of was being upright when I crossed the finish line. When I did, I collapsed. I was spent, absolutely totally spent. They carried me over to a park bench to administer first aid and I muttered, "Did I get a trophy? Did I get a trophy?"

"Yeah," one of them said. "You finished seventh. You finished in the top ten."

I was lying there and every once in a while I opened my eyes to see the lights of TV cameras shining on my face. They were probably using me as an example of how brutal a marathon can be.

All of a sudden I heard my name. "Dick Beardsley! Seventh place!" I didn't care if it killed me, I was walking up there to get my trophy. I made it to the stage somehow and thought, this is just the greatest thing. It was worth it. I was shaking as I accepted the trophy and managed a weak smile. My quads hurt so much I had to walk back down the stairs backward.

I got home, put the little trophy on the table, and drew myself a bath. My dad got home from the game, heard what happened, and was really excited for me. "Gee, D," he said, "I'm so proud of you," blah, blah, blah. "How'd it feel?"

"Piece of cake," I told him.

To myself I thought, I am never running another marathon.

Funny thing about marathons. They must be similar to childbirth in that after a while, all you remember are the good parts. The next one I ran was at the National Junior College Championships in Dowagiac, Michigan, June 17, 1978—the summer I finished classes at Waseca.

Fulkrod had been training us on marathon technique. We did increasingly longer workouts and learned how to drink on the run. A couple of women from the track team posed as water people. They'd take my truck, travel ahead, and set up water stops. I learned to grab the cup and not drink the water until I was back into my stride, then save a little to pour over my head.

The top six runners at Dowagiac became all-Americans

and got a certificate reflecting that. That's the highest honor you could get at my level, other than being a national champion. I wanted it in the worst way.

The morning of the race was sunny and very warm. The course was on rolling hills and the first thing you noticed was the locusts. I can still hear the buzz they made as the day warmed up. This wasn't the best day to run because of the heat, and it wasn't an easy course. I drank a lot as the race progressed.

One of my competitors was Malcolm East from England. He ran for Allegheny Junior College in Pennsylvania. They were tough. They had great cross-country teams, and Malcolm was on his way to becoming a very distinguished runner. He's the one I measured myself against. I'd been getting pretty good on hills, and that day I was right up there in the lead pack with Malcolm and some other guys. I knew anything could happen in a marathon, but I was feeling great.

Maybe it was all the training I'd done with Fulkrod, but going into the championships I knew I was going to love marathoning. As the race wore on, I knew I had a good shot at finishing in the top six. We were running at a sub six-minute pace, and eventually a good gap widened between each of the top few runners. After a while I realized that, unless I dropped out, I was going to be in the top six. I crossed the finish line in third place, at 2:33:06.

Suddenly I was the number-three junior college marathoner in the country! Bill Rodgers, the number-one marathoner in the world, was at the awards ceremony and presented me with my all-American certificate. Someone took my picture with him. It was the best day of my life.

I got home and was so excited I wanted to run another marathon right away. I looked through some running magazines and found one—the North Dakota Marathon in Grand Forks, June 24, 1978. Exactly a week after Dowagiac, and about as long as I wanted to wait.

It was almost midnight when I pulled into town the Friday before the race. I'd spent what little money I had on gas, so I had to sleep in my truck. I set my watch alarm for six o'clock. I was so scruffy I worried they'd turn me away at the registration desk, but they didn't. We boarded a bus and were escorted across the Red River into Minnesota, riding for what felt like forever. We got out to this wheat field where the race started and the whole area was so flat I wondered if I could see Grand Forks twenty-six miles away.

I looked around and there didn't seem to be any ringers. The gun went off and I saw this guy running with a sweatshirt on—unusual in the summer—and he looked like he was pretty good. There was a little group of us at first, but in no time it was just him and me. We talked quite a while. His name was Jim Miller and he was from Grand Forks. Eventually he pulled away from me, but it took a long time. The whole race I thought that my body must be able to recover from marathons pretty well. Here I was in another one only a week after the championships and I wasn't just jogging it out. I was running at a sub six-minute pace.

I finished the race without incident and came in second, with a time of 2:31:50. I went to the awards ceremony at a park and got something to eat at a little barbecue they had. Then I jumped in my truck and drove back to the Twin Cities. On the way I thought, I ran one marathon and finished seventh. I ran another and finished third. A week later I ran another and finished second.

Maybe I could qualify as a late bloomer.

I knew better than to tell my new coach, Scott Underwood, what I was up to that summer. Scott was from South Dakota State University and had been recruiting me for a while. I enrolled at SDSU for the fall semester on a partial athletic scholarship. Coach said he didn't want us to race much, that we should save it for the season. He had cards we sent in once a week over the summer, letting him know how many miles we had put in. I counted my races as regular miles.

Three years at Waseca was more school than I had planned on attending since my goal in life had always been dairy farming. But Waseca had a good agriculture program and I could run. The only reason I continued my studies at SDSU was to run. The thought of having a coach for however much longer was too hard to resist. SDSU had a great cross-country and track program, and had won numerous championships.

I was more into running than ever that summer. When I wasn't guiding fishing trips or milking cows, I was heading out for another run.

The great thing about the cards we mailed to Coach every week was that he summarized them and put out a little newsletter. I didn't know anyone on the team, but I felt like I did from the newsletters. There was a guy, Mike Dunlap, who almost seemed like he was in a contest with me for the most miles. One week I'd run ninety-five miles. The next week he'd run a hundred. I'd run a hundred and five the week after that and, well, you get the idea. That was the first time I ran hundred-mile weeks on a regular basis, but it was such an honor to be asked to join the team I wanted to be in great shape.

When I first arrived at the university it was a little un-comfortable. All these guys were best buddies and I was the new kid. That feeling didn't last long. Within about ten min-utes I started to feel part of the group. Within a few days, I had a new set of best friends. There were seven of us on var-sity, including two sets of twins—Mike and Mark Bills, and Joel and Paul Brandt. Within a week they were calling Mike Dunlap and me the third set of twins, the Dunley twins. We looked alike, acted alike, and almost from the minute we met were inseparable.

After one week, I was gone.

"Where's Beards?" someone asked right away at practice

that evening. I didn't show and didn't show, and pretty soon they checked my dorm room. It was empty. My stuff was gone, my truck was gone, it was like I had never been there.

By then Dad's drinking was about as bad as it ever got, and he was messing with my head. He didn't approve of school, he didn't approve of running, he thought it was time for me to get a job and get on with life. He didn't approve of farming, either, but at least it was a job. He'd been calling my dorm room and arguing with me. If he was so opposed to SDSU, I wished he would have said something earlier, but he just kept yelling at me for thinking running was anything to get serious about.

Fine, I thought, I'll start farming now and be done with school. I'd had it. I just wanted him off my back. I packed up all my stuff and drove home. I was having dinner when Coach Underwood called. The next thing I knew, Dad—who'd been drinking as usual—started yelling at him, too. It got ugly. I took off for a walk and my head was spinning I was so confused.

The next morning I left for Rochester to talk to a guy who said he could help me get set up on a farm near there. It would be my own place. I got five miles from home and thought, this is *stupid*. I was heading south on Interstate 494 when it hit me: I am *not* letting Dad take my dream away. I decided to go back to South Dakota State right then. I made a U-turn on the interstate, drove back to my dad's, and threw all the stuff I'd just unloaded from school into my truck again. "I'm going back to Brookings," I yelled at my stepmom.

I drove eighty or ninety miles an hour all the way back. I'd already missed one practice and had no intention of missing any more.

I walked to the sports complex, went inside, and everybody started hollering, "Beards! Beards! He's back!" Everyone slapped me on the back and told me it was great to see me. I'd known these people a week. Anyone else, you'd think they'd hardly care where I went or if I came back. Not these guys. All was well with the world, now that I'd returned. Coach didn't seem upset at all, just relieved.

I realized I was home.

I took my running to another level at SDSU. I was working out with people who were fired up about the sport, more than any group I'd ever been in. Almost all these guys had been stars in high school and some of them were all-Americans. At first I was a little intimidated, but I soon realized I could hold my own with them. In doing that, I started believing in myself.

Coach Underwood was as good as Coach Fulkrod—or Joe Ross, for that matter—at keeping cross-country fun. We had some great workouts. Underwood would drive us twenty miles out to this little town of White, South Dakota. You had to travel that far to get to a serious hill, and that was still five miles away from one. We ran those five miles to warm up. Then we'd do six half-mile repeats, where we'd run as fast as we could up the hill and use the downhill to recover. After that, we'd run the five miles back to our cars. The workout was known as Killer Hill.

Later in the season, Coach had us run about five miles out of Brookings to a two-mile stretch of gravel with rolling hills. Once we got there, we'd run four miles as fast as we could— twenty minutes—then recover for five minutes. Then we'd run two miles as fast as we could, in 9:30, recovering for five. Then we'd do one mile at 4:35, same thing.

When it was really hot, Coach would have a bunch of great big honkin' watermelons we all cut into after we finished. It was great.

I loved these guys like brothers. It was such a kick to be with people who were as dedicated to running as I was. Everyone wanted to see how good he could become, and everyone wanted to do hard workouts. It used to be difficult to find anyone to run with me in the mornings. At SDSU at least fifteen of us met every morning for a five-mile run. That didn't count the eight or ten miles we did in the afternoons. Coach thought it was great he didn't have to get on us to put in the miles. If anything, he was on us to cut back a little, so we didn't get hurt.

I won plenty of races at SDSU and set my share of course records, but nothing suggested the potential I would demonstrate just three years later. In three years I'd be running marathons at the same pace I could barely hold for six miles in college. Coach sensed my best years of running were ahead of me, so he was heartbroken when I quit school—this time, for good—after four months.

My teammates weren't too thrilled either. "But I'm getting married!" I protested. "My competitive running days are over." It didn't occur to me there was any other way to look at it. I was getting married, we were probably going to have a family, it was time to get a job and get on with life.

I hated to leave. I had more close friendships after four months in that state than I'd ever made in my entire life, or ever would make.

The feeling was apparently mutual. I lived there four months, and in four years I'd be voted South Dakota Sports Celebrity of the Year.

CHAPTER 2

Getting My Hopes Up

I ALWAYS THOUGHT OF MYSELF as a farm kid, even though
I never lived on a farm growing up. We were surrounded by
farms, though, which I loved. There were all these lakes full
of bass and crappies, great trails, and you didn't have to walk
very far to be in the woods. In the fall, during trapping season,
I couldn't be outdoors enough.

I spent most of my free time helping neighboring farmers
with their chores. I fed horses, milked cows, butchered chick-
ens, and cleaned hog barns. Whatever they needed me to do,
I did it and didn't complain. I loved it. I was big into 4-H,
which my parents thought was hilarious. Dad was a traveling
salesman and Mom was a medical secretary. They were city
folk who somehow gave birth to a farm kid.

I had met Mary Hausmann at South Dakota State. She was
from Bonesteel, South Dakota. Her parents weren't farmers,
but a lot of her aunts and uncles were. So when we started
talking marriage, family, and future, the plans were always
set against the backdrop of a dairy farm.

The wedding was going to be in June 1979. Mary stayed
on at SDSU to finish her sophomore year. I became a herds-
man on a dairy farm in January that year. The farm was
near Redwood Falls, in southwestern Minnesota—straight

east of Brookings. I was done racing, but would run to stay in shape.

That's what I told myself, but there wasn't time to run. I got up every morning at four o'clock and never really stopped until long after dark. The place was run-down and I was determined to get it fixed up.

I was miserable. I missed Mary, I missed my friends from school, I missed cross-country. It might have been better had I been getting paid on time, but I wasn't. Plus it seemed like every single piece of equipment on the farm was broken. It was all tied together with bale twine. The silo unloader broke down constantly.

One afternoon there was a blizzard. It was forty below with the windchill and the barn cleaner wasn't working. I was out there with a pickax trying to get it going again and my hands froze around the pickax. I had gloves on, but they were old and they were no match for the weather. I needed help peeling my fingers off the ax and oh, the welts. This sucked.

I got the barn cleaner going and then the silo unloader broke again. I was sitting up there on top of it, bawling. The tears froze on the way down my cheeks.

Crying helped. That's one gift from my parents. They never made me feel ashamed of it. I've never seen *Lassie*—I wouldn't be able to make it through the movie. I can't watch *Bambi*. I can't even watch a lot of TV commercials, I tear up that easily. It's funny, though. No one's ever teased me for being emotional. I've always been this way, and I don't consider it a weakness.

A couple of months went by, and there still hadn't been time for a run. All the energy I used to put into cross-country I was channeling into the farm. I didn't have time to miss running, that's how busy I was.

One night my boss's kid came home from college. "Hey Dick," he said. "I heard you ran cross-country in school." Yeah, I said. "Do you want to go for a run?" he asked.

Well, sure.

We went about four miles and it felt *so good*.

That's all I could think about as we headed back to the farmhouse. I felt so good! I grabbed the mail and there was the latest issue of *Runner's World*. I flipped through it and right away I noticed the qualifying time for an invitation to the Olympic Trials: two hours, twenty-one minutes, and fifty-six seconds. If you ran that time or faster, you qualified for the Trials and got an all-expense-paid trip to Buffalo, New York, for the race.

Two twenty-one fifty-six! That was only ten minutes faster than *my* best marathon time.

What was I doing? I could farm the rest of my life.

All of a sudden I was back in Waseca and Coach Fulkrod was saying, "Dick, I think you can become as good a runner as you want to be."

That was it.

I called Mary. "Mary," I said, "what would you think of this? I'm moving to the Cities. I'm going to get a job at a running store and I'm going to start training. I want to see how good a runner I can become."

"If that's what you want to do," she said, "I'm behind you."

Just like that. The next day I told the farmer, "I'm out of here," and moved to the Minneapolis suburb of Excelsior.

Aspiring actors wait tables, aspiring runners work at shoe stores. A buddy of mine—I used to run against him in high school and college—his dad managed the Foot Locker and gave me a job right away. I was thrilled. There were some great runners working there, including at least one other all-American. I had people to train with immediately and went to work.

I wanted to run Grandma's Marathon in Duluth that summer to try to qualify for the Trials, but wouldn't you know it, it was the same day Mary and I were getting married. The week before Grandma's they were debuting the Manitoba International Marathon in Winnipeg, so I signed up for that. My friend Gordy from Foot Locker knew a bunch of people from the Manitoba Track Club and they took care of most of our expenses.

June 17, 1979. The morning of the race was fairly cool, but not cold. It was calm and clear and the sun was coming out. Runners were there from all over the world. We went out in a big pack and for the longest time ran a sub 2:20 pace. I'd run a 2:31 marathon, but that was it—so this was a lot faster than I was used to.

The lead pack whittled down to about five at seventeen, eighteen miles, and I was in it. Gordy and the other guys I knew had dropped back.

It was a fairly flat course, a few little hills but that was it. At about eighteen miles I was still running a sub 2:20 pace, but I had a long way to go. We were going along and with about four miles left, we hit a long, wide boulevard with no trees. It was very straight. You could see forever.

By that time the sun was up and it was getting hot. I went by what I thought was a water stop where a woman was handing out wet sponges. I grabbed a sponge and was so thirsty I sucked the water out of it. Except it wasn't water! It was filled with soap! *Great.* I was foaming at the mouth. People must have thought I had rabies. And the *cramps!* I had the worst stomach cramps, I was doubling over about to puke, but I kept running. About a mile later I got what I was sure was water and rinsed out my mouth a little bit. The cramps didn't let up, though.

Winnipeg's a big city and we'd been running through a lot of residential areas. Then it was time for the finish in this big outdoor arena. I came through the gates, saw the clock, and knew it was going to be close. I still had to go one more lap around the track, but if I hung on I had a good shot at qualifying for the Trials.

I crossed the finish line. The clock read 2:21:54.

I had qualified for the Trials by two seconds!

I was overwhelmed.

The regional manager of Foot Locker was not impressed. A couple of months after Winnipeg he paid our location a visit and wanted to talk to me. We had a seat right outside the store, on one of those benches they have in the mall.

"You know, Dick," he said, "I want to tell you something. You can really go places in Foot Locker. But it's time you buckle down and really commit to this, because I'll tell you something: You're not going to go anywhere with your running."

I couldn't make eye contact with him, so instead I stared at the pack of cigarettes in his pocket. I pondered life in a striped shirt waiting on people's stinking feet. I thanked him for the talk and quit the next day.

I got another job right away, this time at Sole Sports near the campus of the University of Minnesota. I set my sights on what I hoped would be my next marathon, the Nike/Oregon Track Club race in Eugene, September 9, 1979. At the time it was one of the most prestigious races in the country and I desperately wanted to be in it. There was so much tradition out there, I'd be competing against elite athletes, and it was a good course—flat and fast. That might be the race I could break 2:20. If I did, I might have a shot at some shoes and sponsorship money. Plus I was anxious to run another marathon.

I had no idea how to get to Eugene.

I've never been bashful about asking for help, though. I'd never even met Dennis Frandsen, the father of another good friend. But I wrote him a letter. *Dear Dennis, I'm Dick Beardsley, I roomed with your son Bob in college. I have one goal in life right now, to see how good a runner I can become. But I'm a newlywed, and I'm broke.*

I told him about the race in Eugene, that I'd checked on

flights, and if I could get out there I could stay with a host family and not have any more expenses to speak of. Would his company, Plastech, consider sponsoring me? I could do some promotion for them, wear their logo on my clothes, whatever.

I also told him I'd be happy to consider it a loan and would pay him back as soon as I could.

A week later there was an envelope in the mail with a return address of Plastech. I opened the letter and a check fell out, for the full amount of the plane ticket plus an extra hundred bucks for spending money. *Dear Dick,* Dennis wrote, *I'm glad I can help you out with a dream. Thanks for coming to me and asking. Good luck out there. We're behind you all the way.*

I was so touched I bawled my head off. Someone believed in me!

I flew to Eugene and stayed with a really nice host family. The night before the race I went to dinner at The Spaghetti Factory. There were lots of other runners there, all sitting together in groups. I got a table for one.

The morning of the race was cool, but not cold, and sunny. At the starting line I had my splits—the times I wanted to hit each mile in—written on my left wrist. I wanted to break 2:20. That's what I was there for. The race started and I didn't worry about the lead pack. I just watched my splits and kept hitting them right on. Mile after mile after mile. The closer I got to the finish line, the closer it was going to be as far as breaking 2:20.

I came in at 2:20:22, for forty-fourth place. I was disappointed, but only mildly so. I'd bettered my marathon time by more than a minute, and was happy about that. I knew if I kept improving at this rate, I had a shot at becoming a world-class runner.

I would have a better shot, I realized, if I had a coach. But running was becoming a very popular sport and there were plenty of guys who could run a 2:20 marathon. It was difficult to get anyone to pay much attention to you. I was getting lots of invitations to 10K races, but that was about it.

I didn't have a coach, but I had a book: *Self-Made Olympian* by Ron Daws. It was my bible. I referred to it constantly for workouts. Between that and everything I'd learned from Joe Ross, John Fulkrod, and Scott Underwood, I felt like I had plenty of coaches. I didn't feel like I was in this by myself, not at all. My times kept getting better, so I knew I was doing something right.

Mary helped. She was the best cheerleader I could have asked for. She worked at a bank in those days and we were just barely getting by, but she never complained. Even so, I was anxious to ease the burden on her somehow. When I heard there was a sporting goods show at the Radisson Hotel South, I thought, what the heck? I'd just take a couple dozen copies of my resume over there and pass them out.

It wasn't much of a resume. I had to double-space everything just to fill up a page.

I walked into the main lobby and asked where the event was. Over in the convention center a hotel employee told me. I went through the doors of the convention center and right away a security guy stopped me. "Where are you going, sir?" he demanded. "I'm here to talk to some shoe companies," I told him, not the least bit concerned. "Do you have a button with your name on it?" he asked. Well, no. "Then you can't be in here," he said. The event wasn't open to the public, only buyers.

"Look," I said. "Here's the deal. I'll only be here twenty minutes and I promise I won't hassle anyone. I'll be in and out before you know it."

He grabbed me by the back of my neck, turned me around, and marched me out. "This isn't open to the public," he scolded. "I don't want to see you back here."

I went outside. There had to be another way into the place. It's a huge complex, and I walked all the way around to the other side of it. I checked every door and they were all locked. I kept checking, but no luck. I got to the last door, the one that goes right into the convention center and—it was unlocked! I opened it, not even thinking about the security guard anymore because I was so far from where we'd met.

I opened the next set of doors and there he was, waiting for me and smiling. He grabbed me by the back of my neck again, except this time his grip *hurt*. "If I see you back in here again I'm calling the cops," he snapped.

I was dejected. Still clutching my resumes, I walked all the way back around the complex to where my truck was. I was about to get into it when I took one last look at the main entrance of the hotel. There was an older gentleman walking out and he had something big, something shiny, on his lapel. That was probably one of those buttons the guy was talking about!

My running shoes had holes in them, but even with those ratty old shoes I knew I could go grab the guy's button and tear off running before he realized what hit him. That was just a fleeting thought, of course. Instead I walked up and introduced myself. "Bob," I said, reading his button. "My name's Dick Beardsley. I'm trying to make the Olympic team in the marathon, I need shoes, and I'm trying to get a shoe contract. I have two bucks in my pocket. Would you consider selling your button to me for two dollars if you're not using it?"

"No," he said.

My heart sank.

"I won't sell it to you," he continued. "You can have it." He took the button off, pinned it on my jacket, and shook my hand. "I admire what you're trying to do," he said. "Good luck."

My heart soared.

I walked back into the hotel, but this time through the main lobby. I could see my friend, the security guard, through the dark glass. I opened the door and he saw me right away.

At this point I was holding my resumes so they covered the button, and I locked eyes with him as he approached. I knew he was getting ready to put his meat hooks into me again, and just as he got close enough to, I pulled the resumes down to reveal the button. Oh he was ticked. I loved it.

I got knocked down again real quick, though. All the shoe companies were there—Nike, Adidas, Etonic, all of them. One by one I walked up to their booths and introduced myself. The company representatives didn't make much of an effort to be polite. They just kind of looked at me and mumbled thanks or whatever. As I walked away from their booths, they didn't even wait until I wasn't looking to throw my resume in the trash.

Every company I approached, the same thing.

After a while I had one resume left and there were two firms I hadn't talked to—the Wilson Company and New Balance. Wilson's known for tennis equipment but back then they had a running shoe, too. Which one should I choose? I had no idea. Eeny, meeny . . . and . . . it was New Balance. Fine. New Balance it is, I thought.

I walked up to the booth and read the name tag on the person in front of me. "Hi Mr. DeWaltoff," I said. "My name's Dick Beardsley." I explained my situation. I handed him a resume, and he didn't look put out like everyone else had. He looked it over and said, "You know what, Dick? You have some good goals set for yourself. Your times aren't great, but by golly, every time you run a marathon you get faster."

He looked at me.

"What size running shoe do you wear?" he wanted to know.

I couldn't believe it. The guy was talking to me!

"What size do you have?"

Honest to God, I was so excited I was ready to take any size he had. Finally I said, oh, about 8½ or 9. He went behind the curtain and pulled out a box, this big box of brand-new

New Balance 620s. At the time they were perhaps the number one running shoe in the world. "Why don't you try them on?" he said. Then he suggested I run up and down the aisle a little bit, so I did, past all the people who'd just blown me off. I came back and put the shoes in the box. "Mr. DeWaltoff," I said, "these are the nicest shoes I've ever had on in my life."

"Well, how would you like them?" he asked. "Oh man, would I ever," I told him. "But I can't afford a pair of seventy-dollar shoes." "I don't mean you have to buy them," he said. "You can just have them. And I tell you what. When I get back to our headquarters in Boston, I'll see if I can get you a few more pairs of shoes and get you hooked up with the New Balance Track Club." He took my address. I shook his hand with everything I had and told him thanks. Thanks *very* much.

I floated out of the hotel a different man, and it had nothing to do with the shoes.

Not two weeks later our landlord called the apartment and said, "Dick, you have a big box down here from this outfit called New Balance." I couldn't get down to the office fast enough. I tore open the box and there were eight or ten pairs of running shoes, shorts, singlets, socks, warm-up suits, everything. It was unbelievable.

I went out for my run and I was flying. Someone believed in me besides me! I wore the New Balance logo everywhere. I felt like I did when I donned my cross-country uniform for the first time, except infinitely better. "I'm a runner," I decided. "This is what I do."

The timing couldn't have been better, with the Olympic Trials six months away.

I was running really hard, training really hard, and participating in a lot of local races around the Twin Cities. All I could think about were the Trials in May. But after a while I started to run really badly, and had no explanation for it. We lived in a second-floor apartment and I started to have trouble even making it up the stairs. Maybe I was training too hard.

In March 1980 I ran a 25K race in a really hilly area of Hopkins, another Minneapolis suburb. I went out with the leaders and should have been right up there the entire time, but two miles into the thing I just couldn't keep the pace. I was dragging. I ran by where Mary was watching and told her I was quitting. I couldn't stand it. I wanted to drop out.

"Are you hurting, or what?" she asked. Well, no. I didn't know what it was, but something was wrong. "If you're not hurt, finish the race," she said, giving me the push she thought I wanted.

I kept going, but came in almost dead last. Sixty-, seventy-, probably eighty-year-olds beat me to the finish line.

I didn't know what was going on, but I was sure of this: my competitive running days were over. Moving to the Cities was stupid, as it turned out. I should have been back on the farm. All that work—for nothing! I was washed up before I'd begun and felt worthless. There was absolutely no reason to get out of bed in the morning. What a loser Mary was stuck with. Life stunk.

I moped around the house for a couple of days before Mary insisted: "Go to the doctor and quit dragging us both down." He ran a bunch of tests and finally said, "I think you're anemic." That was *it?* Yeah, he said, suggesting I start taking an over-the-counter iron supplement.

Within a week I felt better than I had in my entire life. Within two weeks I ran some of my best times ever. I didn't even know I was anemic, and still I could put in 100, 120-mile weeks. My racing was lousy, but I never let up on the training. Now, I thought, if I could put in that kind of mileage feeling like crap, imagine what I could do feeling great.

Anemia is common among long-distance runners, or so I've been told. My SDSU coach, Scott Underwood, said he wondered if I wasn't iron deficient in college. Maybe so. I knew it felt like training at altitude versus the way I started to feel now, so incredibly healthy. And I still had a couple of months to get ready for the Trials.

The Olympic Trials were May 24, 1980. It was sixty-five degrees and fairly humid in Buffalo, bad running weather. I had no idea how fast I'd run. The anemia had thrown me off a little bit, in terms of being able to predict much. I went out conservatively, but as the race progressed I started passing more and more people and just felt great. I was really enjoying myself. The course couldn't have been more beautiful. Much of the route was right along the Niagara River.

It was pretty clear by a certain point that I wasn't going to be one of the top three finishers who'd get a spot on the Olympic team. Then again, I was running out of my head. This would be a personal best, there was just no doubt.

Talk about high drama. The closer we got to the finish line, the louder the roar of Niagara Falls. We saw the spray from a long way back, and that's where we finished—right at the Falls. It was awesome.

I'd never broken two hours and twenty minutes, and I came across the finish line in 2:16:01—sixteenth place. To look at my face, though, you'd have thought I made the team. I was crying, I was hugging Mary, I couldn't have been more ecstatic if I'd won the race. To go from a 2:20-plus marathon to a 2:16—I was *so excited!*

I wasn't even out of the chute before I decided I was running four more years. I wasn't going to give up now. My best was definitely yet to come and 1984 wasn't that far off.

Something went off in my head in Buffalo. I could run with the big boys. I went into races more confident. Not cocky, but confident. Invitations to race started pouring in. New Balance sent me more shoes.

To break 2:20 in the marathon is like breaking four minutes in the mile: a very big deal. When I broke 2:20, the confidence it gave me is hard to put into words.

The summer of 1980 I had a couple other breakthrough races. The first was the eighteenth annual Jackrabbit 15 at SDSU, June 7. It's fifteen miles plus 356 yards, this strange distance. Actually it's the distance from White, South Dakota, to the SDSU campus. The Jack 15's one of the oldest road races in the Upper Midwest.

It was fifty-six degrees at the starting line, a cloudy day. "Dick Beardsley! Number one!" I heard, crossing the finish line one hour, fourteen minutes, and fifty-four seconds later—a course record to this day. The reason it was such a big deal is that when I finished, I was still well within myself—and we're talking a sub five-minute pace for fifteen miles. Not only that, but if I could have held that pace another eleven miles it would have been a new U.S. record in the marathon. It's probably silly to think of it that way. Yet, I knew I could have sustained that pace for several more miles. How many, I didn't know. But this was a big breakthrough, in terms of wondering just how much I was capable of.

A month later I ran the fifteen-mile Midnight Madness in Ames, Iowa. It was a really good field of the very top runners. It was hot when we raced, probably in the eighties even though it was dark. I won it in a course record 1:15:10, beating even Frank Richardson—a 2:14 marathoner.

A month later, a breakthrough of a different sort: the Falmouth Road Race in Boston. One of the guys from the New Balance Track Club called me and said, "Dickie! We want to bring you out here. We want to meet you." The Falmouth race is one of the most prestigious in the country. It starts in Woods Hole, Massachusetts, and ends in Falmouth Heights. It's about 7.1 miles, a nontraditional distance, but it attracts the elite of the elite runners.

I got on the plane and Mike Slack was there. Mike was a

top runner from Minnesota and he was with Nike. New
Balance wanted to talk to him about a contract, and he was
running the Falmouth race too. We were talking on the flight
and I thought, this is pretty cool. I was in awe of Mike.

We got out there and who was at the airport to pick us
up but Coach Bill Squires. Squires was under contract with
New Balance. I'd heard of him, of course. He'd coached Bill
Rodgers, for one thing. The three of us walked down the ter-
minal to where the car was. Squires and Slack were talking
and I was following, carrying bags. The little puppy following the big dogs.

The first thing we did was visit the New Balance factory.
They took me down to this room. "Hey, get Dickie some
clothes and shoes and stuff!" one of them hollered. They
filled a couple of duffel bags for me, then took us to supper.
Coach Squires was along and I was wondering when I'd had
more fun in my life. The whole trip was at their expense, and
company representatives wanted to get a good look at me. I
was going to make the most of it. The next day I did a really
hard training run and tried to get ready for the race the day
after that.

The first night we stayed in a hotel, but the night before
the race we were at a house with several runners. There was
a big party, though, and when it was time for bed there was
no place to sleep. We were about five guys to a room to begin
with, and now with everyone crashing, we ran out of beds.
Couches, too, for that matter. Finally things settled down and
it was quiet enough, but I still didn't have a place to sleep.
After a while Coach Squires got up to use the bathroom.

"Dickie!" he said. "What are you still doing up?"

"There's no place to sleep," I told him. "I was just going
to stay up."

"That's crazy," he said. "Here. Take my bed."

"Oh Coach, no way," I told him. "Where are you going
to sleep?"

"I'll find something," he said. "Don't worry about it."

I was so tired, and so anxious to do well in the race, I took him up on it.

Two hours later it was my turn to use the bathroom. I walked in there and there was Coach—in the bathtub! He was sound asleep, covered only by a towel. I hadn't known the guy forty-eight hours, and he would have rather slept in a bathtub than have me go without a bed. I couldn't get over that.

The morning of the race I was more excited than ever, and also wired from the rough night. Warming up, there were all these stud runners that I'd mostly just read about. All these incredible runners, and I was lining up with them! The gun went off and I went out like it was my first race in cross-country—way too fast, destined to fade. Which I did. I finished in about thirty-five minutes. Any other race, that would have been respectable—a five-minute pace and all. But in this one, it put you way back.

I crossed the finish line and the first person I saw was Charlie from New Balance. "Aw Charlie," I moaned. "I'm sorry. I ran like crap today." "Wait a minute, Dick," he interrupted. "We didn't bring you out here for an evaluation. We know you're a good runner. We just wanted to meet you and give you a chance to see what New Balance is all about."

Dejection to elation in less than two minutes. Party time.

I don't drink. I'm determined not to make the same mistakes my parents did. But I'm not above hanging out with people who drink. Which is to say, almost everybody in Falmouth it seemed. I became the designated driver and escorted the group back to the house we were staying at after everyone had partied on. It was fine with me. It was fun to make my way through Boston at night.

It was hard not to think about the Boston Marathon, starting with this trip. The ultimate test for any distance runner is Boston, because of the tradition. It's the oldest marathon in the world, and arguably the most prestigious. I knew if I kept improving, I was going to want to run Boston.

Coach Squires was acting as a chaperone for Mike Slack and
me. The day after the race Mike had other things to do since
he knew so many people in the area. I hung out with Coach.
You talk to anybody, the word *intense* does not begin to describe Bill Squires. From the minute I met him, I thought,
"This guy's as intense as me." That's rare. We hit it off in a
big way. Still, I was surprised by what he asked next. "So,
Dickie, do you have a coach?"

"Well, no, not right now."

"Well, gee," he said, "if you're looking for somebody, I'm
the coach for the New Balance Track Club and I'd be happy
to try to help you out."

Wait a minute. I looked around. Was he talking to *me?*

"Gosh," I said, trying not to sound stupid. He might as
well have told me I was pregnant, that's how much trouble
I had believing this was happening. "That would be *great,*"
I finally said. We were at lunch, and right away he started
scribbling some workouts on the backs of napkins. It was
the start of a very strange and very exciting long-distance
relationship.

I learned quickly that if I had to talk to Coach on the
phone, I'd better do it early in the day. If I talked to him at,
say, eight o'clock at night, I couldn't get to sleep. I wanted to
run the workout right then. He got me so fired up I'd just lie
in bed feeling the adrenaline pound its way through my body.

He sent me workouts all the time, a few notes on torn
pieces of envelope or whatever he grabbed when inspiration
hit. The first six months I was forever calling him, trying to
decipher this or that.

Coach was a fan of high mileage, another reason we hit it
off. I loved his workouts. A lot of coaches will say, "Go out
and run twenty-five miles." Not Squires. You didn't just put
in twenty-five miles. You did fartlek, you did tempo runs,
some repeat miles, all incorporated into the same training
run because it simulated race conditions. I loved that.

There was no doubt, the workouts I got from Squires

were critical to my rise in marathoning. For one thing, he varied them so much they were always fun, always interesting. Running never bored me, but I loved it even more with Squires telling me what to do. I'm an enthusiastic guy to begin with, but Squires took that enthusiasm to a new place.

You know, it's rare to get into a marathon where it's a flat course and you run one steady pace from start to finish. It never happened in my experience. Squires said the more you can get your body used to accelerating, then backing off, then flying up and down hills, then recovering, then sprinting, the more you do this kind of thing in practice, the more ready you are when you get in a race. You're ready for anything.

I met Squires and I started doing 120 miles a week almost immediately. Most days, two workouts—except for Sunday. Sunday I did a long run, usually twenty to twenty-five miles. Then that afternoon I'd do what's called a shag run. It was three miles, just to loosen up my legs from the hard workout that morning and get them ready for the next day.

Squires was big on fartlek. Except his was a timed fartlek. He'd have me do ten times two minutes, with a one-minute recovery. Two minutes of running as fast as I could, with one minute to recover, over and over. I had to run fast during the recovery, too, just not *as* fast. It was brutal.

It was brutal, but I loved it.

I know, I know. You're thinking, what kind of wacko would consider that fun?

But I loved it, I just did. It's been more than twenty years, and I'll tell you the same thing today. I've never been the slightest bit bored by running. You put me out in the middle of South Dakota for a thirty-mile run with nothing to listen to, nothing to watch but the wind blow and—I'm serious— I'd be in heaven. You know why? Because there were . . . mile markers! What objects of reverence, those little posts off the side of the road. They're the key to everything. Between those and my watch, I could design the workout as I went along. It was always different. There was always a new way to push my body to the absolute limit. Of course, back then if you went out for a run in rural South Dakota, every vehicle you saw would stop. The driver was sure you were in trouble. You explained. They thought you were nuts, but headed on down the road.

I don't consider hard work and great fun mutually exclusive. Who decided that anyway? A lot of people say they love running because of how they feel afterward. Not me. Well, I love that, too, but it's also *so much fun* while I'm out there. I used to be able to run thirty miles averaging a 5:30, 5:40 pace the entire time and never be tempted to quit. You start pounding out a couple dozen five- or six-minute miles and you start to feel such a sense of satisfaction and peace you can't believe it. Sure you're tired, sure you're sore, but if you could bottle the high you get from transcending the pain mile after mile after mile, well, you know.

I was out there by myself, I was seeing the country, I was in my own little dream world with no one trying to snap me out of it.

Reality was overrated.

For some time, I'd been looking forward to the next Nike/OTC marathon in Eugene, September 7, 1980. Anyone who ran a sub 2:20 at the Trials got an invitation to run, with expenses paid. It was such a plateau to achieve, when people started paying my way to these races.

My return to the Nike/OTC marked the first time I didn't worry about my splits. Instead of concentrating on my pace, I went out with the lead pack and tried to stay with it.

Which I did, for about half the race.

I finished tenth, with a time of 2:15:11. The top nine runners got an all-expense-paid trip for two to Nike's Honolulu Marathon. Me, I set my sights on a different race. The 1980 New York City Marathon, in six weeks.

October 26, 1980. The New York City Marathon starts at ten-thirty in the morning. It was so cold that day I had socks on my hands. Bill Rodgers was at the starting line, as was Alberto Salazar—it was his first marathon. Bill was going for his fifth consecutive New York win.

The race started and I was right up there in the lead pack. There was a big group of us. We went along, it was still cold, and I was running fast. There were about fifteen of us in this big pack, and just before we went across the Queensboro Bridge the whole group was kind of jostling to one side as we cut corners. Suddenly I was flying through the air, Rodgers was flying through the air, and it felt like I did three somersaults. I got up, I was sore, and my hip was bleeding. The pack was gone.

Still trying to figure out what happened, I looked over to see Rodgers on the ground. Someone helped him up, and off he went. No one helped me, but I got back in it, too.

To read some accounts of the race, you'd think I was just standing there holding my leg out trying to trip Rodgers. To this day neither of us really knows what happened, other than our legs somehow got tangled up together. It was an accident.

Billy, though, he knew to take his time working back up into the pack. Not me. I had such a rush of adrenaline going, I caught back up with everybody right before we started up the Queensboro Bridge. Until then there were the usual throngs of people watching the race, but they don't allow spectators on the bridge. Suddenly it was eerie it was so quiet. All you could hear was the wind blowing through steel and the footsteps of a dozen runners. Slap, slap, slap.

We got to the peak of the bridge where it flattened out for a little bit. I looked around. What the heck? I took off.

I took off, I was leading the marathon, and I thought, this is unbelievable.

The bridge started sloping down and I was coming off of it. I came around the corner onto First Avenue, and it

seemed like there were a million people right at that corner!
It had been quiet on the bridge and now it felt like all of New
York City was out there screaming at the first runner off the
bridge: *me!* The crowd was going crazy, and the noise was
deafening.

I went about three strides on First Avenue, and there was
Coach Squires. His eyeballs—oh!—you knew by looking at
him Dick Beardsley wasn't the person he expected to see!
He started running next to me, screaming, *"Dickie!! What
the hell are you doing? You're leading the New York City
Marathon!!"*

"Yeah, no kidding Coach!!"

He stayed with me, this was at about the sixteen-mile
point, and kept hollering: "Dickie! Dickie! Be cool! Be cool!"
And I thought, you're the one who's getting weird on me,
Coach. "Be calm!" he kept hollering. "Be calm!" I kept running on up ahead as he hollered, *"Go get 'em Dickie!!"*

I headed up First Avenue and had about a thirty-yard lead
or something. Jim McKay was doing the live broadcast with
Frank Shorter—the 1972 Olympic gold medalist in the marathon. They were in the TV truck right in front of me. My
friends at home told me later they were trying to figure out
who I was. "Some unknown runner," they concluded. Somebody checked it out and one of them said, "It's Dick Beardsley from Excelsior, Minnesota." Something to the effect that
I was basically a nobody, and wouldn't be leading very long.

They were right. Within a mile or so a group caught up
with me. Salazar and Rodgers went by me, among others. But
I was still running out of my head.

I finished ninth, at 2:13:55.

Oh my God, talk about elated! It was the New York City
Marathon, I led it for a while, and finished in the top ten. I
went out with the boys, hung with them for most of the race,
and shaved more than a minute off my time.

To be able to say you're a 2:13 marathoner, well, that just
put you in a whole different league. That was so far beyond

what I ever thought I could do. You run a 2:13-something in a marathon, people take notice. I was getting right up there.

That night after the awards ceremony Bill Rodgers walked up to me. "You're Dick Beardsley!" he said. Then he put his hands around my neck, pretending to choke me: "You're the guy who tripped me!" He was laughing and obviously not upset at me at all. I apologized, just in case, probably called him Mr. Rodgers or whatever. But he was cool about it. The item made *Sports Illustrated*. Not the debut in that magazine I'd aspired to, but it's like they say, as long as they spell your name right, just be happy.

The next day I flew into Minneapolis and there was a little crowd at the airport. Some friends were there with banners and the media showed up. I'd finished ninth, but New York City was a big deal. I was becoming a bit of a celebrity.

New Balance started paying me a stipend of five hundred dollars a month. It may as well have been five million, though, because I was getting paid to run. I couldn't believe it! I was never into running for the money—good thing. But to get anything at all for doing something I loved that much—what a feeling!

Now the race invitations really poured in. I ran lots of 10Ks. They brought me in, fed me, and paid me a little something to speak or do a clinic. There was a lot of travel.

"If my running ever starts hurting our marriage," I reminded Mary, "I'll give it up." She appreciated the sentiment, but had no problem with the way things were going. She was still working at the bank and we were still hoping for a family. She came to most of my races if they were in the area, and we were enjoying life.

I took it kind of easy during November 1980. Easy for me, that is. Lots of miles, just no racing to speak of. In December I started building back up. Coach Squires and I decided my next marathon would be Houston, January 10, 1981.

There was a great field in Houston. Bill Rodgers, Jeff Wells, John Lodwick, Benji Durden, Herm Atkins. The who's who of distance runners back then. They put us up in a beautiful hotel. I wasn't used to getting treated like royalty, but I was starting to enjoy it.

The course was mostly on interstate highways that they closed down. We started in downtown Houston, went out, came back into downtown, and went out again. At one point we took a little side route through a park, but otherwise it was all on the highway.

We went out in this big pack and I had one thing on my mind: winning. When I started marathoning I just wanted to hit the times I'd set for myself. As I gained experience, I wanted to stay with the lead pack for the duration. Now my goal was to *win*.

The race went on and the pack started to dwindle until eventually it was just Rodgers and me. I was racing against Bill Rodgers, one of the best marathoners in the world. There was a lot of pressure on him. He was the man. I didn't know what my odds were of beating him, but it didn't matter. For it to come down to Rodgers and me, well, I was running with the gods.

It didn't come down to that, though. With less than three miles to go, there was a little dip and then kind of a gradual uphill. Bill just took off and got a gap on me. I closed it down a little toward the end, but time ran out. I finished the race at 2:12:48, thirty-eight seconds behind Rodgers.

Second place in the Houston Marathon!

Another personal best.

I was ecstatic—2:12! That put me at world-class level.

As if to underscore that point, within days of getting back from Houston, the Japan Amateur Athletic Federation wanted to know if Mary and I would like to come to Beppu. Beppu is the oldest marathon in Japan, and has the same significance the Boston Marathon has here.

I told Mary, "We're going. We may never get another chance to go to Japan." Squires didn't object. "What the heck, go for it," he said. "You recover quickly from these races."

I did. A few days after Houston, I was back doing eighteen-mile runs on hills. People thought it was crazy, but I was so fired up I couldn't wait to get back to training. This was all so new to me. Never in my wildest dreams did I think I'd be running 2:12 marathons and competing against Bill Rodgers and going to Japan. I didn't know how to dream that big.

My good friend Garry Bjorklund—one of the greatest runners to come out of Minnesota—told me it wouldn't last. "You have to be careful, Buddy," he said. "Eventually this will catch up with you." Garry was a high school champion, he ran for the Minnesota Gophers, he was an all-American and an Olympian in 1976. He was one of several people who warned me I wasn't giving my body enough time to recover between races.

Try telling my body that, I thought. I felt great. I didn't want to slow down, not when I was feeling this good.

Mary and I got to Japan a few days before the race and were stunned by the hospitality. The Japanese people we met loved athletics and loved marathoning. They put us up in the best hotel, served us the best food, showered us with gifts, and wanted one thing in return. They wanted me to run my best and if that meant beating all their runners it was just fine. As races go, I've never met people who were nicer. It made me wonder whether if I had punched one of them in the face they wouldn't have said, "Ah, sorry Mr. Beardsley, I got in your way."

It was cool the day of the race, February 1, 1981. We ran 13.1 miles along the ocean and back. What seemed like millions of spectators lined the streets waving their national flags. They only let about four hundred people compete, and the top two hundred or so were elite runners from all over the world. Two of the top entrants that year were the Soh brothers from Beppu, both 2:09 marathoners.

The race started and, as usual, there was a bunch of us in this big pack. You could tell right from the start it was going to be a fast race. The event was broadcast live all over the country, and there were TV trucks in front of us the entire time. Pretty soon runners started falling off.

I'd never run an international race before. Well, Winnipeg, but this was the first time I got in trouble for not knowing international rules. At the first aid station I went by I took some water, then offered some to one of the other runners, who started shaking his head in a panic. Suddenly an official rode up alongside me on a motorcycle and said, "Mr. Beardsley, you cannot do that, you'll be disqualified." That threw me a little.

At one of the next aid stations I picked up two cups. One had some kind of a Coke drink in it and another had water— or so I thought. I threw what was in it on my face and— *ugh!!*—it was some kind of sweet drink too! It was clear, but sugary and sticky. You know how if you get something sticky on your hands you can't wait to wash it off? Well this crap was all over my face and there was nothing I could do. I was only about six miles into the race and things were already starting to unravel. My eyes were stinging and bugs were sticking to my face. I had three miles until the next aid station! I couldn't see, I was spitting out bugs, and I couldn't remember why I wanted to come here in the first place.

Finally, finally, an aid station—and water. Well, let's make sure first. Yep. It was water. I took a wet sponge and wiped off my face. From that point forward I tasted whatever it was before I poured anything on my head.

We were going along and more runners kept dropping off the pace. At 13.1 miles they had cones set up in the street. You went around them and started back. We went through the halfway point in 1:03:12. Not only were we on world record pace, if this kept up we'd break the world record by more than two minutes.

For a while it had been just me and the Soh brothers. The three of us were it, as far as contention for the win.

With about eight miles to go the wind suddenly came up across the ocean and was howling right in our faces. It was like running through water compared to a minute ago, it was that strong. We were going to slow down, I was sure of it. There was no way to keep this pace into the wind.

The Soh brothers got right behind me and I was breaking the wind. That was fine with me, for a while. We could take turns.

They didn't seem eager to take their turns, though. They didn't speak English and I didn't speak Japanese, but surely they knew what I was suggesting when I motioned them to come along. They wouldn't. I kept going, kept trying to convince one of them to step forward, and kept getting more upset. No way was I going to let them suck off me the rest of the race. I started zigzagging back and forth across the road. Back and forth, back and forth. The driver of the TV truck was going nuts. Every once in a while I heard them say, "Ah, Beardsley san, cuckoo, cuckoo." But the Soh brothers weaved right behind me, staying out of the worst of the wind.

We're out here with nothing to break the wind off the ocean, I thought, let's help each other out. When we get within a couple of miles of town, where there are trees and the city blocking some of the wind, fine, it'll be every man for himself. But out here, let's help each other out.

The wind was zapping my energy and they were behind me on a free ride. Forget that. I got so mad I stopped. I actually came to a stop. I let them get a little bit ahead of me, then I tucked in behind them. Finally.

It wasn't long before one of the brothers fell off the pace a little bit. Now it was just me and the other one. Every once in a while I'd check on the one who fell back, though, and sure enough, he was gaining ground. With a mile and a half to go, it was the three of us again and the crowd was going crazy. We were coming into downtown Beppu and I saw Mary riding by me in the press bus. I looked up at her and by then I was really starting to hurt. I was dying. If I could have just had an iced tea with sugar in it, anything that would have given me a little boost.

At exactly one mile to go I had a Soh brother on each side of me. They looked across at each other and . . . took off! Just like that! There was nothing I could do. It came down to a kick between those two at the end, and the one who'd fallen back for a while was the one who won the race. In the last mile they put more than a minute on me, which was incredible.

I came in third, at 2:12:41. When I crossed the finish line I was ecstatic again, though, this time because I was dead. Totally spent. There was nothing left, and I could rest easy knowing I gave it absolutely everything I had.

The Japanese officials were thrilled. They were hugging me and saying, "What a race!" They told me they'd never had a race come down to the last mile like that.

That night they had a huge awards banquet. The vice president of Japan was there, with other dignitaries. The Soh brothers got up on stage and said a few words in broken English. Then it was my turn. I got up there and said, "You know, I can't thank you enough for inviting Mary and me to Japan." "I have to tell you," I added, "I tried Soh, Soh hard." Oh my God, you've never heard such laughter. The place just exploded. It was great.

New Balance had a factory in Japan, and the next day we were going to be flown there. We had a few hours before we needed to leave for the airport, though, so in the meantime we took a taxi to a place called Monkey Mountain, where wild monkeys run around in a park. The taxi drivers in Japan wear white gloves and we were speechless. The cabs were spotless! If a driver was waiting to give someone a ride, he'd take those few minutes to polish up his cab a little more.

We got to Monkey Mountain and I paid our taxi driver.
As soon as he drove off, another taxi pulled up. A Japanese
man got out, walked over, put a wrapped gift in my hands
and said, "Mr. Beardsley, my family and I see you yesterday
on TV running the race, the greatest marathon we've ever
seen in Japan. This is for you from my family. It's a gift because we just loved how you ran. Thank you so much."

We hadn't recovered from that display of affection by
the time we got off the plane and were driven to the New
Balance plant. A Japanese rep from the company picked us
up in a van and radioed ahead so they knew we were coming.
We arrived to a scene straight out of the movies. All the factory workers were lined up on the street in front of the building. We got out and walked between them as they cheered
and clapped. They had a huge bouquet of flowers for Mary.
When we walked inside, the same thing. All the workers
were clapping.

Twenty years later, I can still hear the applause.

We weren't even home two weeks when I got another call.
This time it was New Balance, wanting me to run the first
London Marathon. In less than two months! Mary didn't
even bother to ask for more time off from the bank that
soon, so I went over by myself.

They put me up in a really nice hotel, though the rooms
were tiny, which was fine. A few days before the race I did
some radio and TV interviews, kept training, and did a little
sightseeing on my own. Until recently I'd never been out of
the United States except for a few fishing trips to Canada.
Suddenly I was seeing the world at someone else's expense
because I could run fast! The soundtrack from *Chariots of
Fire* gave me the chills. I didn't think I would ever get used
to this, I was so thankful and awed by the wonder of it all.
This was what it felt like to have a dream come true.

March 29, 1981. It was typical London weather the morning of the race, just the way you imagine it: damp, misty,

cloudy, in the forties or so. We started on a big green, this huge open area. They had six thousand runners in that first annual run, far exceeding anyone's expectations. There were athletes and media from all over the world.

We started in that big field and went through some gates. Then we were out on the streets of London, running through all these historical areas. I still couldn't believe this was what I did for a living! Most guys go out for their morning jog and it's the same old country or city road they've run a hundred times before. My course was straight off a postcard.

The first London Marathon was before they got all the kinks worked out, of course. The route was really winding and for a while it seemed like we were making a turn every block, which slowed us down. There was a blue chalk line to guide us, and motorbikes and a pace vehicle to make sure we knew how to proceed. But it wasn't your typical marathon. The road meandered quite a bit.

The big pack out front started to dwindle.

At about thirteen, fourteen miles, something like that, we crossed the London Bridge. I made a little bit of a move coming off the bridge and a few guys came with me. Then we got into an industrial area of London where the spectators were scarce. Then people really started to fall off the pace. Pretty soon it was just me and Inge Simonsen from Norway. We were running along and the roads were somewhat uneven. They were paved, but they weren't in the best shape. With about three miles to go we came out of a bridge and got onto an old cobblestone road that was rough. It was difficult to run on, and my right calf tightened up on me really badly. Oh, man. Your calf tightens up enough and it can make you stop running, honest to God. After a mile—or what seemed like it anyway—on that cobblestone, we were back on a regular road and I thought I might make it in after all.

With a mile to go it hit me: this was going to be just like it was in Beppu. It was going to come down to the final mile.

The last thing you want in a marathon is to have the race boil down to a sprint at the finish line.

We were going and going and could almost see the finish—it was about six hundred yards away. We saw the crowd and all the banners. It was time. Inge was on my left, and we were both running as hard as we could. We had been the whole race. Neither of us was able to pull away from the other one. Now he was saying something to me in broken English, and I couldn't really understand him. But he had this look like, do I want to go for it? And I knew what he was asking. He wanted us to finish together.

It all happened so fast. I knew one thing, though—it was anybody's race. We were probably going to finish right together anyway. I mean, we were both dying. I was trying to get away from him, and he was trying to get away from me. This race was going to end in a tie whether we wanted it to or not. It wasn't like we decided at twenty-three miles, hey, nobody's close to us, why bust our tails, let's just run in together. That wasn't it. Each of us was trying to bury the other one, and neither of us could do it.

In a spontaneous show of sportsmanship, we grabbed each other's hand and almost in that instant we broke the tape. The photo made papers all over the world.

My first marathon win. Inge's first marathon win. We tied, with a time of 2:11:48. For once my tears of exhilaration went unnoticed, as it was raining champagne.

We got criticized later. People associated with other races congratulated us, then said, you know, it is just not cool to intentionally tie. I did my best to correct the error, but after so much wasted breath I realized people would think what they were going to think.

The cynics prevailed. It's now illegal to hold hands at the end of an international marathon.

The London Marathon is like my first love. Nothing will ever quite compare. Not just because it was my first win. But the people! Years later, after my farm accident, they sent me a few thousand dollars to help with medical expenses. In 1991 they invited us over for the ten-year anniversary of the race. They brought back all the past champions and our spouses, put us up in the best hotel, fitted us with tuxedos, and treated us to a black-tie dinner fit for kings. At the dinner they presented us with engraved watches from the year we won the race, and five thousand dollars just because. Can you believe it?

I can't wait until the twenty-fifth.

CHAPTER 3

The Road to Boston

I WAS A RUNAWAY TRAIN.

That's how it felt. My times were getting so much better so much faster, I had no idea where it would lead. But it was going to be fun finding out.

Once I got my calf taken care of, that is. It bothered me a lot after London. Soaking it, icing it, resting it—nothing helped. A few weeks after the race, New Balance flew me to Boston to watch the Boston Marathon and see a Russian massage therapist they had on staff. He couldn't do anything for it either.

By the time I got back to the Cities, I was bummed. I went to a podiatrist in Bloomington who worked with a lot of runners. He said, "Aw, Dickie, we'll get you fixed up." He taped my foot so when I ran it took the strain off my calf a little. He was so sure this would help he suggested I run ten miles that night, just to show me it would feel fine.

I did, and it worked!

I couldn't believe it. If I kept tape on my foot like that I could still train while the calf healed. What a relief. I didn't say much to anyone about the calf, of course. You don't want your competition to know what's ailing you.

By then Scott Keenan, the race director for Grandma's

Marathon in Duluth, had called. "We'd love to have you run this year," he said. "We'll put you up for a few days, feed you. . . ." He could have saved the sales pitch. I would've run Grandma's the year before had it not been so soon after the Trials.

Coach Squires was fine with it. By then it would be almost three months since the last marathon—a lot of time off for me. Plus Grandma's had a reputation for cool weather—it's right on Lake Superior—and a fast course. Garry Bjorklund ran a 2:10 there the year before.

Every marathon I ran, I knew I had a faster one in me. Even though I'd be spent, even though I'd be cramped up, I knew with a little more training, a little more preparation, a little more experience, I could run faster. That was a fun position to be in. The tables had turned. It used to be I'd see a Garry Bjorklund in a race and almost give up before it started. Now I was the guy people were watching.

Still, everything was happening so fast. Already I had trouble saying no to race directors. They'd call, they'd tell me this 10K or that half marathon would raise money for breast cancer research or some children's hospital. How was I supposed to turn them down?

I knew from the beginning that you're not at the top of this particular game for long. I was going to have fun and race a lot while I could. I didn't know how long the limelight would last, but I wasn't going to waste time indoors if the sun was out.

"You're racing way too much," people were already telling me. "You need to take more time off between marathons. What are you trying to prove?"

I wasn't trying to prove anything. I was having fun, and I was getting faster. What was the problem? Granted, I went at each race like there was a gold medal at stake. It wasn't like I ran one hard, then slacked off the next. Every time it was my best effort. I didn't know how to go at it any other way.

Something would be different about this race. I was sure of it.

Grandma's Marathon was set for June 20, 1981. My last long run was about twelve days before that, twenty-three miles. Coach Squires said, "Okay, Dickie, now this is what I want you to do. I want you to warm up a couple miles, and then I want you to run the first five miles at about a five-minute pace." Now this was a training run! Then he said, "Then I want you to back off for the next five, and then go hard again for the next five and then kind of back off the last five and then the last mile, I want you to run like a 4:45 or something."

I went out and marked myself a course through some suburbs of Minneapolis with plenty of rolling hills.

I warmed up my two miles and went through the next five in twenty-four and a half minutes. I was on a training run with no one pushing me, so that was doing really well. Then I backed off the next five. Afterward, I checked my watch, figuring it would amount to a six-minute pace. It felt like I'd been walking.

I looked at my watch.

A 5:18 pace! That was my recovery. I couldn't believe it. It wasn't like I was strolling along a beach somewhere with Mary, but I was *not* pushing myself. I was intent on doing the workout exactly as Squires had laid it out. I just didn't think either of us realized backing off would mean 5:18.

The next five miles I went hard again and ran a five-minute pace. I was still on hills, I didn't have anyone pushing me, but I felt great. Now it was time to back off again, but again, slowing down was a 5:18 pace!

The last mile I ran in 4:43. I'd been on track for a 2:13 marathon, and this was a training run! I'd never heard of anything like that.

I finished the workout and knew I was ready to pop one.

I called Coach and told him I came through twenty miles in an hour and forty-one minutes. Five-minute pace is an hour and forty. He started screaming into the phone. "Dickie!

What are you doing? *What are you doing?"* He didn't want me to leave it here in suburban Minneapolis.

"Coach, it was a walk!" I insisted. "I wasn't even working that hard!"

"Okay, Dickie. Be calm. Be calm," he kept saying. I didn't answer, but he knew. He knew I was *ready.*

To have done that kind of a workout on hills, in training flats, without tapering down my training at all, well, like I said: something was going to happen in Duluth.

Marathoners wear heavier shoes in training than in racing. When I trained, I wore New Balance 770s. They were a great shoe, really padded, but they're a little bulky. They give you the cushion you need for the constant pounding.

In races I wore New Balance 200s. The company took my foot form and made a customized pair for me. I loved them, but I customized them even more. I ground out the bottoms so the sole wasn't quite as wide. I ground the sides down to get rid of the extra rubber. Then I took a sharp knife like a rug cutter and cut deep into the soles, right up on the balls of my feet. Then whenever I was sitting around, watching TV or whatever, I kept bending the shoes back and forth, back and forth. By the time I finished this routine, they were so light and flexible I could crumple a shoe in one hand.

Warming up before a race I'd be in my training flats. When I put the racing shoes on, a switch went off in my brain. They were ruby slippers. You talk to enough runners, you'll find out how superstitious many of us are. Beyond a certain amount of training, the game's mental—and we all have our little ways of convincing our brain to keep the rest of our body fired up.

A pattern started to emerge before Grandma's. And that was, force me to rest a little—this time, to let my calf heal—and watch me come back faster and stronger than I could have otherwise. I always resisted the break, and I was always thankful for it later.

Now that my last long training run was behind me, the hardest part remained. The last ten or eleven days before a marathon are horrible. You slowly cut back your training, you have so much energy, and all there is to do is wait. I hated the last week before a race, I hated it. It was the only part of marathoning I didn't like.

The last several days I kept cutting down my mileage until the day before the race, when I went out in full sweats and just jogged for about half an hour. That was it. Full sweats no matter how hot it was, so I could just run easy for a little while and still get a nice sweat going. After I was loosened up I'd come back and do about forty-five minutes of light stretching.

Grandma's Marathon is always on a Saturday.

Two days before, I went into my shell. Always. I always did that. There was something about a marathon, I needed about forty-eight hours to go inside my head and stay there. Ask anybody—I'm about as friendly and outgoing as it is possible to be. But you try talking to me within a couple days of a marathon and I'd rather bite your head off than respond.

I left for Duluth Thursday, June 18. Mary had to work, but I needed to be up there for a press conference Friday. I jumped in our little Honda Civic. The starter didn't work, and I always parked it on a hill so I could pop the clutch to get it going.

I took off early afternoon, grabbing the mail before I left. I got on Interstate 35, proceeded north through the Twin Cities, and—I was nervous. That's unusual. I'm Mr. Positive-to-the-Point-of-Oblivion. But suddenly I was filled with doubt. "Maybe I did too many hard runs. Maybe I did too much fartlek. What if I *did* leave my best run on that twenty-three-mile training course?"

The second-guesses were like grasshoppers trapped inside my head. I couldn't stand it. I had to get rid of them. In the mail was one of my running magazines and I flipped it open on the seat next to me, just for the heck of it, even though I was driving. The page it fell open to had this headline: John Graham of England runs a 2:09 at the Rotterdam Marathon.

That was one of the top times ever run in the world! There wasn't much traffic, so I skimmed the article a little bit while keeping one eye on the road.

A 2:09 marathon. Isn't that something?

2:09 . . .

I put the magazine down. I was between Willow River and Moose Lake, Minnesota, on 35, still heading north.

The first mile marker I saw was 209!

I wondered . . .

It would have been silly to think I could run a 2:09 Saturday. Basically I was a 2:12 marathoner, and, well, that was just too big of a leap. But suddenly the only thing I was second-guessing was, how well could I do? I felt the same way I did after that twenty-three-mile workout, like I was going to pop one.

You come down this big hill into Duluth, you see the lake, and you can feel the electricity in the air. One of the reasons Grandma's is such a great marathon is the whole town embraces it. Whether in organization, beauty, or hospitality, this race is hard to beat.

I pulled into the hotel midafternoon and walked to the front desk to check in.

"Ma'am," I said, "do you have a room for Dick Beardsley? Dick and Mary Beardsley?"

"Oh yeah," she said.

"My wife will be coming tomorrow," I told her.

"No problem," she said. "Gee, best of luck in the race Saturday, Mr. Beardsley," she added. "Here's your key, and here's some information for you. Again, good luck."

I told her thanks, grabbed my bags, and walked over to the elevator. The doors were open, and there wasn't anyone around except for the woman who'd just checked me in. I got on the elevator—I was in there by myself—and thought, well, better look to see what room I'm in. The elevator doors closed. I looked more closely at the key and honest to God, I threw my bags down and started screaming. It was room 902!

2:09 backward!

Now there was no doubt. I was going to run a 2:09 Saturday.

I may not win, I thought, but I'm running a 2:09. I didn't tell Mary, I didn't tell Coach Squires, and it was amazing I could even admit it to myself—I'm that averse to trying to predict the outcome of a race. But again, something was different this time.

I was getting more and more superstitious about running, and for these last few marathons I'd been wearing the same warm-ups, same racing shoes, same socks, same everything. For this race, New Balance had new gear they wanted me to wear, with bigger letters so when you're out in front their logo's more visible. I knew I had to wear it, which was fine, but I packed my old racing outfit as a spare. Before a big race there were always nightmares about waking up in the morning, not having my racing shoes, and needing to borrow someone else's that were five sizes too big.

The night before a race Mary and I were always in a room with two beds. She and I slept in one, and—this is how crazy I got—my racing outfit "slept" in the other. Before I turned in, I got everything ready. I pinned my number on the front of my singlet, and placed that on the bed about where it would be if I were lying there. Then I put my shorts just below my singlet, then the socks, then the shoes.

I knew I wasn't going to sleep very well, but I wanted to make sure my racing stuff did.

How crazy is that?

You get to know somebody well enough, you'll find out things about them that either strike a chord, give you the cooties, or both. I don't hear a lot of snickering when I tell runners this story. It's more like a collective sigh of relief. You have to play a lot of mental games to get ready for the trauma of a marathon and, well, whatever it takes.

The morning of the race my body was flushing itself out, as usual. I got into my stuff and Mary and I took off. I was into my game face, big time. I didn't want to see anybody, I didn't want to talk to anybody. We walked out of our room on the ninth floor, the door closed behind us, and—something was wrong.

"Mary!" I said. "I'll meet you downstairs. I have to go back to the bathroom."

I didn't have to go to the bathroom. I was feeling guilty. My old uniform, the one that had been with me through all these great races, was stuffed in a duffel bag in a corner of the closet. I felt like the kid who dumps his best friend when a new kid with better toys moves into the neighborhood. I couldn't leave my good friend stuck in a bag.

I took a hanger and lovingly placed the singlet on it. I found some safety pins and pinned the shorts to the singlet and the socks to the shorts. Then I tied my old racing shoes to my socks. Our window looked right out onto the twenty-five-mile mark. I hung the outfit in the window and thought, by golly, my ol' buddy isn't going to run with me, but he can watch as I go by. Decades later, thinking about this still brings tears to my eyes.

I hung that outfit in the window and everything was complete. I was ready. I wasn't before, but I was now.

"Promise me you will never tell *anybody* about this," Mary begged, when she discovered the outfit later. And I didn't, until that fall when I ran a half marathon in Thunder Bay, Ontario. I was giving a speech, I got to telling stories, and it just slipped out. Joe Henderson was there from *Runner's World*. The next month he recounted the story in a magazine, accompanied by an illustration of the outfit hanging in the window.

But I'm getting ahead of myself.

I got downstairs to the lobby and Mary wanted to know if I was ready.

Yes.

It was a perfect day to race. About forty-five, fifty degrees, no wind, a little fog, and overcast. There were plenty of good runners, but the media had been focusing on Garry Bjorklund, the defending champion, and me. The gun went off, we started running, and after about a quarter mile I looked over my shoulder. Garry was beside me, but I couldn't see anyone else. Maybe that was the fog. Nope, Garry said, it's just you and me, Beards.

Garry—most of us call him BJ—had a big hometown advantage because the town of Twig, where he grew up, is right outside Duluth. He was running in front of hometown fans, a year after winning with a 2:10 and putting Grandma's on the map. So it was hard to believe what happened next. "Listen," he said. "I'll stay with you as long as I can but it's your race, man. I'll do my best to help you." This was crazy. Had God sent this guy to me?

We were going along, and after about four miles I got something like a bear-trap stitch in my side. It was hurting so much I could hardly breathe and it was affecting my running. I wondered if I should tell BJ. You'd never say anything like that to Rodgers or Salazar because they'd probably just take off on you, but BJ just told me he was there to help me, and I trusted him.

"Oh Beards," he said. "Listen. There's an aid station in about a mile. We'll just cut back the pace a little bit. You can get a drink of water and rub it out and you'll be fine." Which is what happened. And off we went.

I had no idea why BJ was being so nice to me. I never found out, either. He was kind of into himself a little bit and I was in awe of him. Why ask? I guessed he didn't think he was in the best shape. I was the young kid, the hungry one, and was in top form.

As we ran, I followed this blue line they'd put down. I

basically stayed right in the middle of the road. The course meandered some and BJ cut the corners. If there was any little curve he took the shortest route. I took the road right down the middle.

After I don't know—what, seven miles?—he said, "Beards! Listen. If you keep running the way you have been, you're going to end up with about 28 miles instead of 26.2. When they measure these courses to certify them, they take the shortest possible way a runner could. That's the only way a course qualifies for certification." I listened. "Man," he said, "if there's a curve, take the inside edge. If there's a place where you can cut at an angle, do it. You'll save yourself some time and energy." I kept thinking, this guy's great. I was still so new to racing these things needed to be pointed out.

I kept glancing back every once in a while but there was just no one behind us. We were going along, chatting a little bit, and came through the halfway point in about 1:04:36. "Hey Beards," BJ said. "You have a 2:09 going." He didn't say "we."

I wasn't thinking about a 2:09 seriously anymore, not at the halfway point—no way.

We kept going, and it was getting harder to keep chatting. The race was starting to take its toll a little bit. At about eighteen miles you come up across the Lester River and start getting into the edge of town. I was feeling good and it seemed like BJ was feeling good, too. Was he ever. I kind of glanced over my shoulder again and by the time I looked back around, BJ was about fifty yards in front of me, flying.

Part of me wanted to yell, hey BJ, I thought this was my race. Then it dawned on me, he probably didn't realize he was in such good shape. Maybe he never considered he'd be up in the lead at this point, running this fast.

If he got into city limits with the lead and got the crowd hollering for him, it was over. The crowd can take a runner who's not in perfect condition and propel him beyond what he thinks is possible. If BJ got into town with a little bit of a lead, I might never catch him.

I panicked. I took off like a jackrabbit.

I caught up with him. I wanted to get rid of him before we got into town, so I took off again. I opened up a gap. A reporter for the St. Paul paper rode up alongside me on his bicycle and said, "Beards, you just ran a 4:42 mile," or whatever it was. Pause. "But BJ's only about twenty yards behind you." Oh man. He was hanging on. I took off again.

Now we were between twenty-one and twenty-two miles and the reporter was back beside me, telling me I just ran a 4:37 mile. "And man," he said. "BJ's hurting." I looked at him in disbelief. "*BJ's* hurting?" I said. "*I'm* hurting!"

By now I was worried I'd blown my wad. I cut back a little bit and could see I'd broken away from BJ. Finally. I came around the corner and saw Lemon Drop Hill. It's the only big hill on the course. It's not all that long or steep, but it comes at about the twenty-two-mile point, a tough spot in any marathon.

I was coming down on the back side of it, and it was a long, gradual downhill. At that point I had a pretty good lead going. I got about halfway down and—there was Joe Ross! All that encouragement in high school—he was much of the reason I was even here. He had his street shoes on and was wearing long pants, but he was running beside me hollering, "Dick! Dick! *You're doing great! Keep it up!*"

From that point forward I had no idea how fast I was running. My watch had stopped! Back then there was no paint on the road to tell you what mile it was. Mile markers were little sticks in coffee cans filled with sand, but it was misting and they were hard to see. Many of them had gotten knocked over. I had no idea where I was on the course. Obviously I was getting close to the finish line because the crowd was getting thicker and thicker and noisier and noisier.

I got down to the bottom of this gradual downhill where it flattens out and all of a sudden the bear trap was back. The side ache! It was back, only worse—maybe five times worse than it had been at the beginning of the race. I could feel my stride shrink. It felt like I was pulling an anchor. I must be running about a ten-minute mile, I thought. I wasn't, but it felt like it. Now I was hurting so badly I didn't even know if I could finish.

I looked back, and couldn't see anybody behind me. I kept running, but I thought each step might be my last.

I got downtown where all the big buildings are and could see the Radisson off in the distance. I knew when I hit that I'd be about a mile from the finish.

The crowd was getting thicker still, and noisier still.

I came to a corner where we had to take a left by the Radisson. I still had this terrible cramp, but I looked up—and there was my outfit hanging in the window! It was such a warm feeling, such a hug, such a boost of confidence.

With about a mile to go I saw this little kid up ahead of me, playing in the street. I thought, well, he'll get out of my way.

I got closer and closer, and started looking for options because he was still sitting there, playing. There were people on both sides of the street. I looked to the right and there were spectators. I looked to the left and—more spectators, plus a big light pole. I was also surrounded by a few dozen people on bicycles. This was before they had much in the way of crowd control.

"Get the kid out of the way!" I screamed. Nobody was doing anything! I was about twenty yards away at this point, still running at a good pace.

"Get the kid out of the way!"

He stood up, and his eyes locked on mine. We were about ten yards apart. He stood there frozen, looking at me. Just as I tried to decide which way to go around him, even though there was really no room, he decided to go that way, too. We both guessed wrong. I ran right smack into him, and he went flying into the crowd. I looked back and saw him crying, so I knew he was okay.

Meanwhile my cramp was *gone*.

That's bizarre. I had this terrible gut ache, I ran into this kid, he went flying, and my gut ache disappeared. It's like he took it with him.

I had less than a mile to go. I got to what they call the DECC—the Duluth Entertainment Convention Center. It's a big arena. I was going around it and had no idea how close I was to the finish. I had no idea how fast I was running. There weren't any clocks around. I got to the one last turn, ran to the right, and it's one of the greatest finishes in marathoning. It's about a quarter mile, maybe six hundred yards, something like that—one straight shot to the tape. There were thousands of people on both sides of me. They were moving in and it was awe inspiring. At this point I was sure I'd win the race. I got closer and closer. At the finish line there's a big clock. Any moment now, I'd be able to make out what it said.

It was reading 2:09:04.

That wasn't right. The race officials must have forgotten to start it on time! It was way behind. I didn't know how fast I was running, but it wasn't that fast.

I heard the announcer as I got closer. I was about fifty yards from the finish, the crowd was going crazy, and the announcer yelled, "Dick Beardsley! He's going to break two hours and ten minutes!" The crowd was going absolutely, totally wild. The announcer said it again: "He's going to break two-ten!"

I came across the finish line leaping for joy, my arms in the air. I was hollering, I was screaming, I was crying. "Dick Beardsley!" the announcer yelled. "Our 1981 Grandma's Marathon champion! Two hours, nine minutes, thirty-six seconds!"

My mom and dad were there. Neither of them had seen me run a marathon before. Mary was in the chute with me. Everyone I knew, everyone I loved, they were all there. Race officials were crowding around. Scott Keenan, the race director, had tears streaming down his face. Mom and Dad were crying. My sisters were crying. Mary was crying. Everybody was crying.

My official time was 2:09:36.6, so it went into the books as 2:09:37. A course record. It's still a course record.

The officials grabbed me, put blankets around me, and with the help of a few police, escorted me to a tent where there were lights, cameras, a thousand questions. That bedlam finally subsided a little bit and we went back to our room. The phone was ringing off the hook. People were calling from all over the country. I just wanted an outgoing line. I wanted to talk to Coach.

"Dickie!!" he said, unable to contain himself. *"I knew you were going to do it, Dickie!"* Pause. "Open the envelope."

A week ago he had mailed me an envelope. When I had opened it, there had been another envelope inside that said, "Open after the race."

I tore it open and there it was. "Dickie," Coach had written. "I knew you were going to run a 2:09."

I was bawling my head off.

The course length controversy started right away. Charlie Rodgers, Bill's brother, was quoted as saying the course must have been short. Bill was the top dog in marathoning, you have to remember, and anyone on his tail was suspect. Charlie's the nicest guy and a friend of mine now, but back then we didn't know each other.

They remeasured the course, and it was 150 yards *long*.

A hundred and fifty yards! I could've come in another eighteen seconds or so faster, at least! The American record would've been broken.

I'm told a course is never *exactly* 26.2 miles. They have to pad it slightly. You'd rather have it a little long than too short. This way my time counted. The other way it wouldn't have.

New Balance promptly bumped my stipend up to a thousand dollars a month. The phones never let up. I was always doing a radio or TV interview, when I wasn't racing. I set my sights on the Boston Marathon the following April.

The folks in Oslo, Norway, brought me over to the Bislet games in July. It's one of the biggest track meets in the world. All these great athletes were there. Herschel Walker—one of the top 100-meter runners in the world—and Carl Lewis. I was sitting at a table eating breakfast with these guys!! I won the half marathon in 1:04:10, on a hilly course. I pulled away at about nine miles and didn't have anyone breathing down my neck as the race progressed, so I was really pleased—to have just come off a 2:09 marathon only the month before.

It was in Norway that I met the race director for the Stockholm Marathon. "Would you be interested in coming over?" he asked. "Bill Rodgers is. We'd love to have you. We'll bring you and your wife. We'll pay you to come, and pay you more if you do well. What do you think?"

Mary was all for it. Coach Squires said, yeah, what the heck.

The Stockholm Marathon was August 15, 1981.

We flew from Minneapolis to New York City and changed planes. They put us in first class. It was Bill Rodgers and his girlfriend, Amby Burfoot from *Runner's World* and his wife, and Mary and me. Whose life was this? It was still so hard to believe this was happening to *me*.

They told us that to counteract jet lag, instead of taking a nap when we arrived, we should just stay up and then sleep when night came. We got to the hotel and of course the first thing I did was go for a run into the city. It was two days before the race, so I was only going to go eight miles or so. Except I got lost! By the time I got back to the hotel I'd gone about fourteen miles. Oops.

I took my shower and had a little something to eat. The phone rang. It was Bill Rodgers! Bill Rodgers called *me*. "Hey

Dickie!" he said. "I just woke up from a nap. Do you want
to go for a run?"

I thought, *he* called *me*. Bill Rodgers called *me!* I was *not*
turning this down. The chance to hang with Bill Rodgers—it
would be like some basketball player shooting hoops with
Michael Jordan. Bill was one of the top marathoners in the
world, but the thing I loved about him was that he was just a
regular guy. He was always accessible to the reporters or fans
wanting a piece of him. I respected that.

We ran. Eight miles! It was two days before the race, and
I'd just run twenty-two miles. For a lot of people that would
have been suicide, but I didn't worry about it at all. The only
thing that bothered me was getting lost.

The Stockholm Marathon's unusual in that it starts in the
early afternoon. It was sunny and warm on race day. The gun
went off. We were on the Olympic track in Stockholm and
made a loop or two. Then we went out on the streets and
there was a big pack of us. Just before twenty kilometers—
12.4 miles—we came up on a bridge. There were probably
half a dozen of us in the pack now, including Bill Rodgers
and Inge Simonsen. We started coming up this long bridge,
this long hill, and I just took off.

I opened up a gap on everybody, a big gap. I broke away
from everyone, including Rodgers. Once I got ahead a little
bit, I looked back and could see Rodgers pulling away from
the others. I knew eventually he'd work his way up to me.

Which he did.

He caught up with me just as I recovered. I'd done a hard
burst, but I was ready to go. Rodgers was beside me and I
thought, I could just take off right now. But here he was,
huffing and puffing. He said, "Dickie, we got 'em broke.
They're broke. We broke 'em." He was still trying to catch
his breath when he said, "What we ought to do is just kind
of back off the pace a little bit and recover because they're
not going to catch up with us."

I *had* recovered! I should have just taken off. But you

know, this was Bill Rodgers. He talked me out of it. I was such an idiot.

I didn't realize that right away. At the moment I was feeling great, my buddy Bill and I leading the Stockholm Marathon. There were throngs of people lining the streets and TV cameras watching our every move.

At about sixteen miles I hit a little bit of a bad spot. I wasn't surprised. I knew somewhere between sixteen and nineteen miles it was bound to happen, but it didn't worry me anymore. I knew I'd work through it and be fine. At the moment I wasn't fine, though, and Rodgers must have sensed it because all of a sudden he just took *off*. He took off and I never saw him again.

I finished in 2:16:17, the first time my marathon was slower than my last one. The streak was over, but it still got listed by the Guinness Book of World Records: thirteen consecutive marathons with each one faster than the one before.

I finished second behind Rodgers, who came in at 2:13:28. I crossed the finish line and I thought, Dick, you blew it. He got you to slow down just long enough for him to recover.

I had a lot to learn.

It was inevitable that I didn't have a personal best with every marathon, though. When I got my 2:09, there were only four guys in the world who'd ever run faster. In Stockholm, the officials were delighted with my performance. At the banquet, the race director walked up and said, in broken English, "Dick, you did really well." He handed me an envelope. "Here," he said. "This is what we agreed on."

I stuffed the envelope in my pocket. Mary and I kept dancing.

We got up to our hotel room a while later and I took the envelope out. Inside was eleven thousand dollars, in crisp, one-hundred-dollar bills. I was shaking. I threw the cash on the bed. I'd never seen that much money in my life.

Before we headed back to Minnesota, New Balance took

Mary and me sightseeing for a few days. They had a big sail-
boat and we sailed for a couple days and slept on the boat. It
almost took being trapped on the water to get me to take a
day off from running.

I hadn't been back from Stockholm very long when my now
good friend Dennis Frandsen—my college roommate's dad—
made me a very attractive offer. How would Mary and I like
to move into a cabin on the St. Croix River, rent-free, while I
trained? Would we! I'd do some promotions for his company,
Plastech, which made injection moldings.

The log cabin was a hundred years old, just the greatest
place. It was fifty miles north of the Twin Cities, on the bor-
der of Minnesota and Wisconsin. There were forests everywhere, and all kinds of trails perfect for training.

Technically I was a spokesperson for Plastech but I wasn't
required to be in the office much. They paid me about eight
hundred dollars a month. Mary got a job at the Century 21
office in nearby Rush City right away. Between our jobs and
my New Balance stipend, we were finally able to start saving
money for the farm we wanted to buy someday. We got really
involved with our church and it took about a week to decide
we were home.

Squires was having me do the same kind of training I was
doing before Stockholm—intense workouts, sometimes 140-
mile weeks. Making the 1984 Olympic team was still the goal,
but it was too early to think about that much. The Boston
Marathon was the more immediate focus.

By now I had an invitation to go back to the New York
City Marathon, but I was weighing that against an offer from
Montreal. Montreal had a big marathon, too, and they were
offering me twenty-five thousand dollars just to show. It didn't
matter how well I ran, I got that much money just for showing up. New York was the better race in terms of exposure,
but I'd had plenty of that. Montreal it was.

Mary's folks joined us at the cabin for Labor Day weekend. It was kind of cool and I wore a nylon running suit when I left for a workout. I started at our cabin and went about six miles into town, then headed back to our place. I was about three miles from being finished, running by a farm, when three dogs came out of a cornfield at me! A German shepherd, a Doberman, and a big farm dog charged at me as I flew down the road. They knocked me over, sending me head over heels into a big heap. They bared their teeth as I screamed, *"Somebody help me!"*

I zipped my jacket up as far as it would go, thinking for sure they'd lunge at my neck. I was already bleeding. There was gravel ground into my knees and arms. I kept screaming, *"Somebody help!"* A lot of times when you make such a commotion, dogs will back off just from the shock. These didn't, and nobody was coming out of the farmhouse.

I was lying there kind of dazed. Slowly I rose to my feet. For some reason the dogs stayed put. I backed away from them gingerly, took a few steps, and jogged away ever so slowly.

I got back to the cabin and was furious. Where was my shotgun? I love animals, but was only going to love these dogs after I'd killed them.

My in-laws calmed me down. We called the sheriff's office. There wasn't much they could do, they said. They'd go over to the house and tell the people to keep their dogs chained up.

The next day I was a little sore on my run, but didn't think anything of it.

Two days after that I was in a little five-mile race in Grantsburg, Wisconsin, just across the river from where we lived. I won it in 25:05. By that afternoon I could hardly walk.

The next morning I could hardly get out of bed. My back and hip hurt so much all I could do was sit in a whirlpool. I called Dr. Arne, my chiropractor in Wayzata, and started seeing him every day for the next two or three weeks. He worked on me for two weeks before he said, "Okay, you can go out and jog a little bit but make sure you sit in a hot tub first to get loosened up." He cautioned, "As soon as it starts to hurt, I want you to stop and just walk back."

Every day I could go a little farther, and eventually the pain subsided.

It was into October now, though, and I'd missed too much training for Montreal. There was a twelve-mile race coming up at the end of the month, the Halloween 20K. It was from downtown Minneapolis to the capitol building in St. Paul and it would be a good test to see if I was healed.

It was really cold on race day. I got into this—dog fight— with a runner from the Twin Cities. We were on a five-minute pace, but there was wind and sleet and ice in our faces the entire time. Everything hurt from the waist down. I was glad I hadn't tried Montreal.

We were dead even as we raced toward the finish line. I outleaned him at the end and won. But oh, it hurt. I wondered if those dogs hadn't sucked my best racing years right out from under me.

I got off easy.

The following spring, I learned, a little kid was out riding her bicycle in front of the same farmhouse. The same three dogs went after her and mauled her. She was hospitalized with serious injuries, but survived.

Then they put the dogs to sleep.

You do enough running, dogs are always something to contend with.

In the late fall of 1980 I was out one morning just as the sun came up. As I passed one house, two little wiener dogs started chasing me down the road. I went up a hill and one dog quit, but the other stayed on my heels. Suddenly a car crested the hill and hit the dog following me. I looked back and there she was, dead.

It was my fault. Most of the time if a dog's chasing you, it'll run away if you stop and turn or pretend like you're going to pick up a rock. But no. I was running and wanted to keep going. The car came up over that hill and the dog was toast.

I was heartbroken. I couldn't even go back and scoop it off the road, I was that sick to my stomach. I showed up at the shoe store later that day to work, but was still so sick I took the rest of the afternoon off. It got to me so badly I didn't run that particular route for *months*.

One spring day before Grandma's I went back that way again. It was so pretty out there, and I'd finally healed from the trauma. I went down the same road and suddenly this little wiener dog tore out of the bushes and bit me in the calf! I was bleeding and I was stunned.

A woman came out of the farmhouse in a housecoat.

"Coco!" she hollered. "Get *over* here!"

I stopped, shook the dog off my leg, and had to ask. "Ma'am," I said, "didn't this little dog get hit by a car last fall?"

"Oh yeah," she said, "but we saw it happen. We got out there right away and got her into the vet. The vet didn't think she'd survive, but she did."

"Thank you," I told her, six months of guilt spilling out in tears of relief. This dog had every right to bite me! I'd left her for dead. I hadn't even gone back. She'd just nailed me in the calf, and I wanted to let her munch on the other one, too.

"Has she had her shots?" I asked the woman.

"Oh yeah, she's fine," she said. "Sorry about that."

"Nah, there's nothing to be sorry about."

After that, if I was going to be running in a certain area a lot, I'd go up to the houses with dogs and get an introduction to them. Once the animal sniffs you a little bit, it knows you're okay. If I was on an unfamiliar route and saw a dog up ahead, I'd stop and pick up a couple of rocks. Usually just the threat of that was enough to scare the dog off.

I haven't had a run-in with a dog in a long time now.

The Houston Marathon was January 24, 1982. Race officials had invited me back since I had won second place the year before. I didn't look at Houston as an end in itself, just a way to train for Boston. I'd been training the same way I did every winter, early in the season. Lots of miles, a lot of strength work, not much speed work. No sense getting into peak form in January. There would be no way to hold it until April.

Houston was uneventful. A large pack went out, as usual, and as usual, it dwindled down. It kept dwindling down until eventually it was just Benji Durden and me. Durden made the 1980 Olympic team and he was a 2:10 marathoner. With three miles to go it was still just him and me. Coming back into the city for the last time he said, "Hey Dick, do you want to just help each other out for a while? I'll lead for a while, then you can. We can take turns." We did that for a couple miles, but then it was his turn to take the lead again and I just couldn't keep up. I fell off the pace a little bit and finished second, with a time of 2:12:42.

I was happy, especially considering all the training I'd missed. I won eight thousand dollars for my effort.

The next month I flew to Atlanta to start training for Boston.

People thought I was down there to escape the cold weather, but that wasn't it. Boston's hilly and so is Atlanta. There weren't many hills where I lived. The only way to train for a race like Boston, Squires told me, was to run on hills. Being where it was warmer was a bonus.

Mary and I shared an apartment with Mike Demperio. Squires got me hooked up with Mike. He was a runner and was single, so Mary started cooking and cleaning for both of us. A really good marathoner, Dean Matthews, lived nearby and I started training with him right away.

I was on the phone with Squires constantly once I got to Atlanta. My running was going well. We decided that about six weeks before Boston I'd run a 30K race in Japan. Thirty kilometers is about 18.6 miles: perfect. It was just the right distance to see where I was at with my training. Mary went back to South Dakota to visit her parents when I left for Japan.

I had to fly to Dallas to make a connection to Tokyo, and on the way I felt a sore throat coming on. I was congested and thought, this is not good. By the time I got to Tokyo I was really, really sick. I got some cold medicine before I checked into the hotel, then went for a run, trying to loosen up the phlegm. When I got back I started the shower and ran the water so hot the whole room felt like a sauna. Nothing helped.

Race day came and I was wearing a bib with the number one on it, probably because of my Grandma's Marathon time. This was a big deal race. It was on TV, people were lining the streets, the usual fanfare. I was about halfway through the race and—I couldn't breathe! I was so sick and congested, I dropped out.

The folks from the Japan Amateur Athletic Federation, who'd invited me over there and paid my way, were really nice, but I was bummed. Here it was, six weeks before Boston, and I was in a stall mode again. I got back to Atlanta and felt like crap, still sick. Squires said, "Dick, you'd better get to the doctor, maybe you need some penicillin or something."

I found a doctor in Atlanta and he took some chest X rays. He got them back, studied them for a few minutes, and got this *look* on his face. "Uh, Dick," he stammered. "I think there's something wrong with your heart. It's all enlarged." I couldn't believe what he said next: "I think you'd better quit running for a while."

It wasn't my heart, I thought, it was my lungs—because suddenly I couldn't breathe again, and it wasn't because of a cold. This could not be happening.

I found a pay phone right away and called Coach. "Dickie!" he said, like, get a *grip*. "Of course your heart's enlarged! You're a marathon runner! Take those X rays to another doctor. Find one who works with athletes."

"Oh yeah," that one said. "Your heart's just fine."

Well, now it was.

Squires suggested I run once a day for a half hour to forty-five minutes. "Take it slowly," he said, "and just get your strength back." That was difficult! The only assignment I was ever given that was next to impossible to fulfill was holding back.

You'd think I would have welcomed the rest, but I didn't. I just didn't. I was possessed by running. I didn't feel good about myself unless I was out there training, constantly.

Finally after a couple of weeks I was up to about ten miles a day. I felt good, but Boston was less than a month off.

The next week there was a 10K race in downtown Atlanta. Dean Matthews was in it, as was the guy who beat me in the Houston Marathon, Benji Durden. The course was really hilly. I finished in 29:12, my best 10K ever.

I won the race.

It was called "The Heart Run."

Once again the break had been good for me. I felt great. Stronger than ever. *Ready.*

It really helped to have Dean to train with. It was especially helpful on the long track workouts. We'd do repeat 800s or quarters or miles, and one guy might lead one lap and the other guy the next.

Another thing that helped were my regular visits with Dr. Dave Martin, an exercise physiologist. He was associated with the Athletic Congress, and I got hooked up with him after the Olympic Trials. I was seeing him a lot, making sure I was in top form.

Still another thing that helped was having nothing to think about except Boston. I was training full time. I was breathing, eating, sleeping Boston. After Boston it was just an abyss—that's how much I was putting into this one race. It was as if the world would end, one way or another, there.

I went for a run right away every morning. Then I came back, ate, maybe got a massage or sat in a hot tub. Then I ate a little more, took a nap, and went on another run. I came back, did some stretching, lifted some weights, and sat in a hot tub again. Sounds like an easy life, doesn't it? Not the way I was doing it. The runs were long and hard, the workouts brutal.

Dean and I would go to the track and do these . . . ladders. We'd run a three- or four-mile warmup, then get on the track and do a couple of 200s. Then a couple of 400s, a couple of 800s, a couple of three-quarter miles. Then we'd do a mile, then back down the other side. It was just a short jog in between each sprint, and when it was all finished we ran a mile in about 4:30.

Does it still sound easy?

Dean and I weren't racing each other. Squires didn't want us to. He had times he wanted us to hit instead. It was a very intense, but very controlled, workout. We'd finish, we'd be breathing heavily, but we were well within ourselves. Each of us knew we were in the best shape of our lives.

Every night after dinner I went for a walk for about a half hour. Sometimes Mary came with me, but if she did, I went on another walk by myself later. The walks were a new addition to my training regimen, but they quickly became as important as the long runs. It was time to think, think, think about the task ahead. Meditation. The hills took so much out of me that I needed to walk just to get my legs loosened up and ready for the next day. I didn't walk far or fast. But it helped quiet my mind.

That wasn't easy to do.

If I let myself think about how much the Boston Marathon meant, I'd go nuts.

Then again, maybe I already had.

On one of my walks I found a rock. It was round and flat, but there was a piece missing, so it was in the shape of a V— V for victory, I decided. Every night on my walk I stopped. I took the toe of my right shoe and put it in that V. I made sure the rock was where no one else would ever notice it, so it was

right there the next evening when I could touch my shoe to it
again. Just another of what was becoming a number of rituals
that helped me believe this race would be my best ever.

Two weeks before the marathon I flew to Boston to stay with
Squires and finish training. I got there on Saturday. Sunday,
Coach drove me out to Hopkinton, where the race would
start. He dropped me off and said, "Dick, just run fifteen
miles—but cruise. Run easy, be in control." The main thing,
he said, was to just take it easy.

Away I went. Right away he started yelling at me: *"Dickie!
Slow down!"* I tried to pull back the pace a little, but it felt
like I was floating, it was that effortless. He followed me in
his car and kept hollering at me to slow down. After a while
I couldn't even hear him. I was in a different place.

He drove up beside me.

"Dickie!" he shouted. *"Just relax!"*

"I *am,* Coach!" I told him, coming to a little bit. "I feel
like I can fly!"

I couldn't believe it when he told me I was running a 5:20
pace. No way, I thought. I was doing an easy run. It felt like
a jog.

I must have been in better shape than either of us realized.

The next day a nor'easter hit and that night I could hardly
run five miles because the snow was so deep. The day after
that I was supposed to do a killer workout on Heartbreak
Hill, up one side and down the other—eight times. "Dickie,
forget that," Coach said, looking out the window.

"No way, Coach," I told him. "I'm doing the workout."

"I don't even know if I can get you there," he said. Heartbreak Hill was twelve, fifteen miles from where he lived.

"Please," I said. "Just try."

We bundled up and took off. He got me within about
three miles. That was fine. I wanted to warm up that far
anyway.

"Okay, Dick," he said. "When you finish, go over to the college and take a whirlpool, and I'll meet you there."

I made my way to Heartbreak Hill. By now it had warmed up to the point where there were ice pellets mixed in with the snow. I ran on the frontage road that paralleled the main street and then started the first of eight trips up and back. The road was really icy and I couldn't run nearly as fast as I wanted to. That was the least of it, though. My eyes were burning they hurt so much. I literally had to run with my eyes closed.

Up and down I went, just as *hard* and as *fast* as the wind and the snow and the sleet would let me. I was running the workout just the way Coach had planned. Well, not as fast, but the effort it took with the storm at full force was like nothing I'd ever attempted.

I'd never worked this hard *in my life*.

All I could think about was how there was *nobody* else out running in this crap! Salazar and Rodgers were probably training where it was warm, like any sane person would. Not me. I was out there on Heartbreak Hill in a honkin' snowstorm. There was *nobody* this tough!

I finished the workout and was fired *up*.

"I'm ready, Coach," I said matter-of-factly. *"I'm ready."*

I still had one more long run to do, though, and I couldn't do it in the snow. Coach sent me back to Atlanta for that. Mike was going to pick me up at the airport, but it would be a while. I put my running stuff on and threw my bags in a locker. I did a thirteen-mile run from the airport and talk about flying! I'd been running in the snow with sweats on. To be out there in shorts and a T-shirt, I felt like a little bird flying around, scoping out the airport neighborhoods.

I stayed in Atlanta until a week before the marathon.

By then the snow was gone in Boston and the grass was greening up. New Balance wanted me to accompany a bunch of guys to Lawrence, Massachusetts, where they were having a big race later that year. We ran part of the ten-mile course and some local TV stations got some footage. That night we did a big running clinic and everybody was excited about the marathon.

Rodgers would be there. They said he was in great shape. By now it was also official: Salazar was coming. He'd just been in a 10K duel with Henry Rono—a Kenyan and one of the world's fastest runners. Rono outleaned Salazar to win it. Salazar's time was 27:30, more than a minute and a half faster than my best 10K.

Thursday night before the race I was in my hotel room watching TV. They had live coverage of Salazar getting into town because he grew up out there. "Alberto, why did you choose Boston?" they wanted to know.

"I looked at the field and I didn't really think there was anybody who could beat me," he said. "Everyone wants to be a Boston Marathon champion, and that's why I'm here."

Salazar had a reputation for making bold claims. The thing was, he delivered. I took what he said seriously.

On the other hand, I thought, you son of a buck, you are not invincible. So long as you're a human being, I told myself, you can be beaten. I didn't discuss this with anyone, but I remembered what I'd heard so often: the marathon has a way of humbling people.

How did Salazar know he wouldn't be the one getting humbled Monday?

I didn't know what he was up to when he talked to the press the way he did. If he was trying to intimidate me, it had the opposite effect. I was more focused than ever, wanting to prove him wrong about the field.

There was a big press event at the Lenox Hotel on Saturday. Rodgers got his number—one. Salazar was two, and I was three. Salazar didn't show up for this. I talked to the press, but that was going to be it for a while.

Now I hid, like I always did before a race. Before I'd been fine, going out, signing autographs, doing whatever I needed to do. But now I was withdrawn, really withdrawn. I was so withdrawn I didn't even want Mary around. Well, I wanted her with me—but I didn't want her to say anything. She knew that. She was my shadow. If we were out somewhere having a meal, she took care of the people who came up and said hi. I didn't even recognize them, that's how much of a zombie I was. "Oh, don't worry about Dick," Mary would say. "He's in his pre-race mode."

I went out the backstairs of the hotel for my runs, trying to sneak out without anyone seeing me. Sunday it was rainy and windy and cold. I was glad for the excuse to have my warmup jacket zipped up to my mouth and a stocking cap pulled down so far over my forehead it was hard to identify me. I was so into getting ready. The physical work was finished, and now it was just mental preparation—which for me meant absolute, total withdrawal from human contact.

The reason is it takes a lot of energy. Some people will say hi, how are you, and hope you answer "fine" so they can be on their way. I'm not like that. I don't blow people off. I make time for them, and a quick hello often turns into a twenty-minute conversation. The thing was, just before a marathon, I had to conserve. All my energy had to go into the race, it just did.

I knew Boston would be the most important race of my life. It was the Boston Marathon! All the tradition, the laurel wreath, all of it—it was the reason I'd been able to think of nothing else for the last six months. Make that the last six *years*.

My whole life boiled down to this. One way or another, this race would change everything. I was standing on that precipice.

About five o'clock Sunday afternoon, someone wanted to throw me off of it. There was a knock at the door. It was Pete Squires—no relation to Bill—from Adidas. I knew Pete, I'd run with him. "Dick!" he said, "Grete Waitz is upstairs. She and Jack want you to come up and visit for a few minutes.

They just want to talk to you, wish you well, that sort of thing." That's odd, I thought. I'd just visited with Grete the day before, at the press conference. She was the number one women's marathoner in the world. She'd won the New York City Marathon three times in a row, and would go on to win it six more times. I knew her husband, Jack, and considered the two of them friends.

Still, it was the night before the race.

"No."

That's what I should've said. But I had trouble saying it, especially to someone like Grete. I told Pete I'd come up.

I got there, and suddenly she and Jack had me in a corner, telling me what a good company Adidas is. Grete said she'd been running with them for years and they treated her really well. They paid her well, they had a good product, blah, blah, blah. Pretty soon another guy came up and I thought, they're trying to brainwash me.

"Well, Grete, nice chatting with you," I said. "I have to get going."

I wasn't back in my room twenty minutes when there was another knock at the door. It was Pete again. He said, "Dick, here's the deal. I want to offer you something."

"Pete," I said, "I have a big race tomorrow. I don't want to be talking about contracts."

"I know your contract with New Balance expired April first," he said.

Didn't he hear me?

He asked if I was still with New Balance.

"Of course," I told him. "They're just waiting to re-sign me, to see how well I do here."

"Here's the deal," he said. "You wear our clothes tomorrow in the race, our clothes and our shoes. I'll pay you twenty-five thousand dollars right now and no matter how well you do, after the race we'll sit down and I promise you we'll write you up a great contract."

I was flabbergasted.

I looked at him. "Pete," I said, "first of all, even if I wasn't with New Balance, it's the night before the race. The last thing I want to worry about is how much money someone's going to pay me. Second, New Balance took a chance on me when I was a nobody. I went to you guys, I went to Nike, I went to everybody else, and all of you slammed the door in my face—except New Balance. Do you think I could show up tomorrow on the starting line in Adidas clothes? Can you imagine what they'd think of me?"

I felt like I was in Bedford Falls and Potter had just offered me a job. I didn't need to think it over, I didn't need to talk to anyone.

"No thanks," I said. "I could never live with myself."

I closed the door without waiting for him to answer.

The nerve! There were so many Adidas athletes in the race. Was he trying to break my concentration? Twenty-five thousand dollars was a lot of money back then—it still is. Maybe he was hoping I'd be thinking of that instead of the race.

If so, he underestimated my concentration.

I didn't have nightmares on the eve of Boston, but I was really uneasy. I was drinking water, juice, whatever, all night long, and all night long I was up going to the bathroom. You have to be hydrated. Mary was sleeping in the other bed. I was tossing and turning so much she wouldn't have gotten any sleep otherwise.

I didn't have butterflies in my stomach. These were wasps. They were wasps, and they wanted *out*. I was going crazy. I turned out the lights at midnight and thought, oh my God, I still have *twelve hours* to wait.

I couldn't stand it.

CHAPTER 4

The Boston Marathon

THE CALENDAR SAID APRIL 19, 1982, but that's not how
it felt. It felt like it was Christmas morning and I was five
years old. Remember when you were a kid, you went to
bed Christmas Eve, you knew Santa was coming, and you
couldn't *wait* to get up to check what you got? That's how
I felt. I was so excited, I wanted to run the race the minute
I woke up.

I opened the blinds, expecting to see cool weather, maybe
some rain. That's what they'd been predicting. We were supposed to have a tailwind and I thought, man, this is going
to be great. But it was a sunny day, not a cloud in the sky. I
turned on *The Today Show* and there was Willard Scott, talking about what a great day it was going to be for the Boston
Marathon, with temperatures in the seventies. I thought, great
day for a marathon? Obviously Willard Scott has never run
one! Seventy degrees is hot, especially in Boston this time of
year, especially for runners not used to the heat.

Boston's unusual in that it starts at noon. Most races start
in the morning. Usually I didn't eat before the race, but it was
only seven-fifteen and I knew I was going to need something.
I had some toast and watery hot chocolate from room service.
I kept hydrating myself, downing fluids constantly. I drank

this stuff called Gatorload, which they say is like eating twelve plates of spaghetti. It tastes terrible.

The waiting really got to me. I could hardly stand it. The anticipation! I was so full of energy after tapering down my training and loading up on carbohydrates. I was *possessed* by this race.

Finally it was nine-fifteen and time to meet the New Balance people, who'd take me to Hopkinton, where the starting line was. It was 26.2 miles from the Boston Sheraton, race headquarters, where we were staying.

Mary didn't come with me. She was going to stay at the hotel and watch everything on TV. You have a better view that way. I gave her a hug and a kiss. She wished me well. She didn't say much. She'd been through this before.

I got down to the lobby and it was packed. So many people were hollering, "Dick!" and patting me on the back. I thanked them and wished them good luck, too, even though I desperately wanted to stay in my shell. Finally a New Balance guy rescued me. We got to the car, a station wagon. They were hauling about ten guys, and by the time everyone else piled in, the only place left for me was the back compartment. The rest of the guys were all about 2:25 marathoners. I'd run a 2:09, so I half expected one of them to say, "Dick, here, you ride up front," but no one did.

I was so crammed in between luggage and the back window I had to keep my knees bent way up the whole hour-long trip. The back window wasn't working and they couldn't close it. Exhaust fumes were rolling in. I was getting sick to my stomach. Oh Lord, this was not good.

Then my positive side kicked in and I thought, there must be a reason for this. At least I was by myself back here, and that was good. Everyone else was yakking and laughing, but I could stay in my shell. No one could even see me with all the duffel bags piled everywhere.

I thought about the race. I thought about Mary. I thought about my dad. Dad wasn't an athlete and never saw me race until after I got out of high school. But now one of the reasons I was here was the high school graduation present he had given me, a handwritten certificate good for one round-trip ticket to the Boston Marathon. He said maybe someday I'd want to run Boston.

That was when I was a nobody. I'd always been described as an average or less-than-average runner in high school. But Dad had heard of Boston and knew it was the premier event for runners. Now here I was, not just running the marathon, but I had the second-fastest time coming into the race. I wasn't just running, I had a chance to win it.

I kept thinking about Dad and almost started crying. I tried to think of something else.

We got to Hopkinton and New Balance had arranged for me to be at a certain woman's house. I had my own room and bathroom. She had other runners around, but I had my own space, which was wonderful. It was probably about four blocks from her house to the starting line, and it seemed like there were millions of people right in this neighborhood.

Ten-fifteen. I met the woman, thanked her, then went up to my room and stretched out on the bed. I listened to music—Dan Fogelberg's "Run for the Roses," stuff like that. I kept drinking, drinking, drinking, probably going to the bathroom every five minutes I was drinking that much.

Eleven-twenty. I went outside and jogged around a little bit to warm up, but stayed away from everybody. Then I came back and did some stretching.

Eleven-forty. I drank a quart and a half of water. I could feel the water sloshing around in my stomach, so I knew I'd had plenty to drink.

I never left quite early enough for a race. It was somewhere between a quarter to and ten to twelve. I came out of the house and looked up to where the starting line was supposed to be. There were about seven thousand runners competing and every single one of them was in front of me. I panicked. I thought, oh my God, I'm not going to be able to get to the front before the race starts. The gun would go off and all this hard training would go to waste. Honest to God I almost started crying. I wanted to scream. I ran through the crowd. I didn't throw people out of my way, but I showed them my number three and told them I had to get to the front. Everyone was really nice. "That's Dick Beardsley!" they started hollering. "Let the guy through!"

It was like the parting of the Red Sea.

I got to the front in plenty of time, maybe eight minutes before the start. But now I had this uncontrollable urge to go to the bathroom. Suddenly the eight minutes weren't enough. I busted through the crowd and found a tree and just went. There were all these spectators around, but I went anyway, I didn't care what anybody said.

I got back in line, took my T-shirt off, and threw it into the crowd. Now I was ready. I looked to my left, and Salazar was there. We didn't acknowledge each other. Bill Rodgers was on my right. We shook hands, and wished each other luck.

They had a big rope stretched across the starting line. I thought, oh man, they're going to drop the rope and it's going to wrap around me. I was freaking out. Because at this point I couldn't stand it anymore. I couldn't wait for the gun to go off, honest to God.

I was standing there, going crazy with anxiety, when the announcer said, "One minute to start!" Suddenly I felt a tap on my shoulder. I looked back. It was this buddy of mine, Barney Klecker from Minnesota. Barney was a good marathoner. He said, "Dickie! Did you double-knot your shoes?"

"Barney," I said. "I never double-knot my shoes. Just forget it. They'll be fine."

Now there were forty seconds left. I felt another tap.

"Dickie!" Barney insisted. "You'd better double-tie your shoes!"

"Barney!" I snapped, "I'm not double-tying my shoes. Leave me alone! I'll be fine. Good luck." But I was ticked off.

Then it got to me and I thought, oh man, Barney's a good

friend of mine. He was just trying to help me out. I turned around to tell him thanks, I'll double-tie my shoes—but he wasn't there. I looked down and there he was, double-tying my shoes *for* me! I couldn't believe it.

The announcer said, "Fifteen seconds!" By now Barney had finished with my shoelaces. People were inching ahead and I was screaming for someone to get this rope out of the way. With ten seconds to go, they finally dropped it.

The gun went off, and it was like Salazar was shot out of a cannon. He took off like Carl Lewis in the hundred-yard dash. I was right with him. I was right on his butt. The first half mile was narrow, downhill. We were flying.

You have to fly at first, to get away from everyone else. Because the last thing you want to do is get tripped, have someone catch your heel, have your shoe come off . . . you'd be screwed for the rest of the race.

We got to the bottom of the hill and there was this little kid with a cup of water. I thought, what the heck. It wasn't an official aid station, but it was hot and I wanted water right away. I tried to grab the water and the kid pulled it away from me. Great. This was going to be good. Now there was another kid offering water. I reached for it again, and this one pulled it away too. What? Were they saving it for their dads? Maybe they got scared.

We went through the first mile in four minutes, thirty-eight seconds: suicidal. There was no way anyone could hold that pace, but I knew it was going to be like that and I had practiced it in workouts. To go out hard, then sit back a bit.

We were going along and I felt like crap. It was hot, my feet felt awkward, I felt bloated. I'd been drinking so much I felt waterlogged, but I hoped that would help me toward the end.

At about three miles I thought, this might not be my day. My feet were burning, really burning. I found out later a retired anesthesiologist—Dr. Alex Ratelle, who was running the marathon—took a temperature reading of the pavement

at the ten-mile mark and it was 105°. No wonder my feet
were hot.

There was a big pack of runners, dozens of us. I was up in
the lead pack. I wasn't leading, but at this point I didn't want
to be. I just wanted to get comfortable. At about five miles
we went by a lake and there was a guy and a gal out there ca-
noeing. Rodgers tapped me on the shoulder and said, "Hey
Dickie! Wouldn't it be nice to be out there right now?" I
laughed. "Man, would it ever!" Salazar didn't look like he
was feeling very well, but I didn't think anyone was.

I knew if I gave it enough time I'd probably start feeling
better. At about six, seven miles I started to find my rhythm.
I felt better, and my feet weren't hurting like they had been.

We were going along, I was feeling good, and these guys
started doing surges. I thought, oh man, don't start doing this
stuff now. Salazar apparently thought the same thing because
he said, "Those dumb asses! Look at those—" and he got
upset.

The thing with surges is, they get everybody excited. Pretty
soon, someone else goes, then someone else. You can't get left
behind. You have to go with them, too. And on a hot day,
you have to conserve early on. We were running fast enough
as it was.

Every mile that went by, another guy dropped off. We got
to about ten miles and were running well under a five-minute
pace, but I felt good. I was comfortable.

It seems like nobody works in Boston on Patriot's Day.
They all come to watch the marathon. Today was a perfect
day for spectators. They estimated the crowd at two million.
People were ten and twenty deep on each side. There were
parties, bands, everywhere. You ran by Wellesley College
at about the halfway point and the girls—it was an all-girls
school—were going nuts. They were screaming so loud you
could hardly hear anything at all. I got pumped. I fed off
crowds. They helped me a lot.

We went through Framingham, the town where Salazar

grew up. There was a Nike store in the area and he ran for Nike. There were signs everywhere and people leaning out of the windows hollering, "Alberto! Go get 'em!" They were screaming. All of a sudden he looked over at me, then looked back at the crowd and started waving to everyone on his side of the course.

I thought, you're not going to get to me. Two can play at this. I nudged Salazar so he looked at me, then turned toward people on my side of the course and waved to them, even though they weren't cheering for me. I looked back at Salazar and he looked ticked.

When you had two guys like us who were so evenly matched from a conditioning standpoint, it was a mental competition: a chess game.

I offered Salazar water a lot. He never offered me any, but then, he hardly ever took any for himself. I think from about the point we broke away from everybody else, every time I got water I offered it to him. I wasn't trying to get to him by doing that, like I was so confident I could afford to help him out. It was just that it was so hot. I took water every chance I got.

I kept a sponge tucked in my shorts during marathons. I'd take one drink, then maybe pour another one over my head. Then I took another one to pour on my sponge. I'd learned that if my legs started to go dead I could just squeeze the sponge, feel the water run down my legs, and be refreshed. It felt really good.

At about fourteen, fifteen miles, almost everyone had dropped back, and we were down to four runners. Salazar, Rodgers, Ed Mendoza, and me.

We came down a big hill at about fifteen miles, and Rodgers took off. I followed. At this point, you had to go, even though there were still ten miles left. You couldn't let anybody get way out in front. The four of us surged ahead, we got to the bottom of the hill, and started up another long one. As soon as we started up, Rodgers dropped right back.

We climbed that hill and at seventeen miles took a sharp turn at one of the fire halls. Then we were on the road that took us into downtown Boston. That's where we started what were four major hills on the course, culminating in Heartbreak Hill—the big one everybody talks about.

Just before we turned, I knew Rodgers was finished, at least as far as contention for the win.

Now there were three of us. Salazar, Mendoza, and me. I looked at Salazar, I looked at Mendoza. Mendoza looked good. He was hardly sweating, he was up on his toes, he looked fresh. We took a right turn at the firehouse and it was like Mendoza stepped off the edge of the earth. He was just gone. He dropped out of the race, right there.

Now there were two. Salazar and me.

Everybody had been talking about how it was going to come down to a two-man race, Salazar and Beardsley. That's hard to predict, though. Of course, Salazar knew I was probably the one he'd have to worry about. I knew he was the one I'd have to beat.

We made the turn at the seventeen-mile mark and started four miles of hills. The crowds were unbelievable. There was no crowd control. After our race they finally got some, but that day there was none. As we went through the hills, there was maybe enough room for Salazar and me to run side by side if we would have wanted to, but that was about it. People on each side of the street could have reached out and touched people on the other side. That's how close they were. It was so thick with spectators you couldn't even see how the hills went up. It was just this mass of humanity, people hanging out of trees or whatever. And the noise!

The bedlam took my mind off the hurt. We were both starting to feel the effects of the race.

My goal going into the marathon was, if I could get to the top of Heartbreak Hill at twenty-one miles and still be in the lead or within striking distance, I'd have a good shot at the win.

We were running through those four miles of hills faster than anyone had ever run through them before. I put the hammer down. I tried to bury Salazar. I wanted him to hurt bad. I knew he *was* hurting, but then I was, too.

Going into this race, Salazar had never had anybody with him in a marathon after sixteen miles. He'd always been alone the last ten miles after breaking away from everybody.

Now we were at the top of Heartbreak Hill and I was thinking, okay, Salazar's never been in this spot before. From about the ten-mile point I'd been leading, but never by more than a couple of strides. Salazar wasn't able to control the race and I knew he was just hanging on.

Then again, so was I.

The thing that got me through all the hills was thinking I could lose Salazar, but it hadn't worked. Coming down off Heartbreak Hill, I got to the bottom and thought, man, he's still here. I got dejected. There were about five miles left and it was getting tough to stay focused.

The crowd helped, though. They were going nuts. It seemed like everyone had a radio. They'd never seen a race where at twenty-one miles two guys were running together. People were hanging all over the place trying to see where we were, sirens were blaring, and it was exhilarating.

I got down to the bottom of the hill and my legs were dead. I couldn't feel my legs from the waist down. They were numb. If I have to stop and tie a shoe, I thought, I won't be able to get going again. My legs were on automatic pilot. Something was telling them to put one foot in front of the other, honest to God.

Oh man, five miles left. Five miles to go in a training run was nothing. But in a marathon, it was forever.

I thought, Dickie, you have to get that out of your mind. Forget you have five miles left. You know even if you're hurting bad you can go at least another mile. I decided to try something. I was talking to myself, out loud, though not so loud Salazar could hear.

"Okay, Dick. You've come this far. You're in the lead. All you have to do is run one more mile."

One more mile, I told myself.

I finished mile twenty-two and got to twenty-three.

"Okay, Dick. You're still in the lead. One more mile. That's all you have to do."

Just one more mile.

I reached mile twenty-four. It was working!

I was hurting bad, but I knew Salazar had to be hurting just as bad—because he was never able to just spurt ahead. We were both hurting.

We were killing each other. I'm serious.

I had no idea how fast we were running. Didn't care. It didn't matter. I had no idea we were running at record pace. In the last few miles I'd been able to tell where Salazar was without looking back because I could see his shadow. Every time I saw his shadow I picked up the pace a little bit, and didn't let him go by me.

All of a sudden I saw this huge shadow and I thought, what, did Salazar eat his spinach and turn into a big Popeye or something? I looked over my shoulder and it was a press bus. Coming straight down the middle of the street right behind us. They had to get to the finish line before we did, but the crowds were so thick they had to plow right through where we were running. The bus hit my shoulder as it went by. I was ticked.

Salazar had seen the bus coming and kind of cut behind it. I was so upset I punched the bus. I found out later Salazar wondered why I got so mad, wasted energy and all that. But it scared me. By the time I saw it, it was right on my shoulder. I was venting, and it felt good.

The bus threw diesel fuel back and the crowd kept the fumes in. I was still in the lead.

About a half mile down the road, all of a sudden this guy in a big long coat came out and grabbed me and tried to stuff something in my pants. I didn't know what he was doing.

Then the guy stuffed some money into Salazar's shorts. This was weird. I was just a farm kid from Minnesota. What was going on?

Now we were about a mile and a half from the finish line. The crowds were so thick we almost had to run single file. There was so much noise my ears were ringing. It was like standing on the ground next to a jet airplane about to take off. My ears hurt. I couldn't hear myself think.

Salazar and I were running along so close. As close as I'd ever want a guy to be. He was right in my back pocket.

Twenty-five point two miles.

That's what it said on the pavement in front of me, in bright blue and yellow paint: "25.2 miles. One mile to go!"

Oh my God.

My God, Dick, you have one mile to go and you're going to win this race!

I couldn't stop thinking that. I knew Dad was at home watching everything on TV and suddenly I started crying. I thought of my high school graduation present, the tears were streaming down my cheeks, and my legs were turning to rubber.

"Dick!" I thought. "Get a hold of yourself!"

I literally shook myself and said, "Dick! Get *into* this! Don't be thinking about that!"

Now the crowd was really going nuts. I was hurting, but I was pumped. I knew Salazar was also. With about a half mile to go I had the biggest lead of the race and it was about two strides. It wasn't much, but at this point, it may as well have been a mile. And I thought, Dick, this is it. Salazar doesn't have a big kick, but it's better than yours. You have to go for the win right now.

A half mile to go.

I pushed off with my right leg, and all of a sudden I got a charley horse in my right hamstring. You could see the knots bulging out of my leg. I couldn't run! Well, I could run—but the leg was useless, and I slowed down a little.

Salazar flew by me and I thought, oh my God. I started crying again.

I thought, my God, I've come this far only to get a charley horse?

For about the first time in my entire life, I wondered, why is this happening? I got selfish. I thought, there are thousands of runners out here. Why is this happening to *me?*

I couldn't see Salazar anymore. The motorcycle cops were blocking my view of him. They thought I was out of the race, that it was just going to be Salazar now.

I was doing the best I could, running, but I couldn't push off with my right leg. All of a sudden—I didn't see it—it was probably the only pothole they missed, but I stepped in it. Obviously I wasn't expecting to. But instead of derailing me further, it jerked my leg out. I could start running again!

I had my stride back!

I looked back, and didn't see anyone coming. I looked ahead, and could see only the cops, not Salazar. I knew I could probably walk the rest of the way in and still get second place.

But I also knew I'd never be able to live with myself if I didn't go for the win.

I put my head down and started pumping my arms. Never before and never since, I felt myself go into a gear I didn't know existed. Suddenly it felt like I was on a cloud, flying. Like angels had grabbed me by the shoulders and were carrying me. I kept pumping my arms, my head down.

Now there were only a few hundred yards left. We came around this corner and turned right, onto Hereford Street. I could see the cops around Salazar. But he was maybe twenty yards ahead of me.

Suddenly this twenty-yard lead went down to ten.

Then five.

Just before the top of the hill on Hereford Street we made a left turn, and had about a hundred and fifty yards to the finish. The turn was a good place to check on your opponent because you could just glance over your shoulder.

We came around this corner and I wove my way around motorcycles. They were *everywhere*.

We went around this corner, Salazar looked over to see where I was, and I was right in his *face*.

You'd have sworn he saw a ghost. Oh, the look of *horror* on his *face!*

He thought I was out of it, but I was *right there*.

A hundred yards to go.

It was him, a motorcycle, and me. Salazar saw me, but the motorcycle cop didn't. As we turned left, the cop—instead of going with Salazar—kind of turned to the right to try to keep the crowd back, and didn't see me. He thought I was way back. We made this left turn and the cop cut me right off. I practically had to jump over his front tire to get to the other side of his bike.

I caught back up with Salazar with fifty yards to go.

Which was nothing.

The motorcycle broke my concentration. Salazar and I were about dead even when I jumped over the bike. Until then, I'd been a shade behind, but gaining on him. Now suddenly my concentration was off, Salazar went into his kick a stride and a half before I did, and that's how we finished.

We both broke the course record, we both broke the American record.

Salazar finished in two hours, eight minutes, and fifty-one seconds. I ran two hours, eight minutes, fifty-three seconds.

I was ecstatic—and disappointed beyond belief—*at once*.

I thought, my God, I just ran a 2:08 marathon and I'm getting second place! The police grabbed me and I was crying: "Man, what do you have to do to win this race?" I got over it real quick, though. Salazar was looking for me, and I was looking for him. We hugged. "Dick," he said, "I've never had anybody push me as hard as I was pushed today." That was the biggest compliment I'd ever had about my running, and to have it come from the world record holder! I said, "Man, you ran a great race."

If Salazar wouldn't have been there there's no way I would have run a 2:08. John Lodwick got third and his time was 2:12:01. Rodgers was fourth, at 2:12:38. The winning time should have been closer to one of those, given the conditions. But Salazar and I were both so stubborn.

Neither of us ran this well again. We didn't give an inch, and about killed each other in the process. Seriously. I was never the same again, running, mentally or physically.

Some people say it's a bigger deal to win the Boston Marathon than to get a gold medal in the Olympics. In Hal Higdon's book, *Boston: A Century of Running,* he says the 1982 duel between Salazar and me is one of the most memorable races in that marathon's history, if not *the* most memorable.

When I see a videotape of the race, I think of how much fun it would have been to attend as a spectator . . . just to watch. Let alone be in it. Even watching a tape today, it makes the hair on the back of my neck stand up. Squires did some TV commentary and you could hear him hollering, *"Dickie! Dickie!!"* They were broadcasting from the top of a six-story building and he came within an eyelash of falling off of it, he was so excited.

Right away it was time for Salazar to be pulled up to the podium to get the laurel wreath. They took him over. I had to walk by the podium also and was right behind him. They put the laurel wreath over his head when he got up there and the mayor held his hand up.

He grabbed mine with his other hand and held it up, too.

Salazar needed medical attention right away. He was hurting. I was okay, so they took me into the garage of the Prudential Insurance Company building, which was right at the finish line. The room was filled with media, and there was a big table set up with bright, bright lights all around.

Now I was the little kid at Christmas again. Except the presents had been opened and I was showing them off. People were firing questions at me one on top of the other and I was grinning big and yakking nonstop. Salazar was off somewhere with IVs in him. I was in front of the press with the limelight to myself and loving it.

Everybody had questions about the motorcycle. I found out one of the announcers broadcasting the race had said, "The motorcycle's got to get out of the way!" To read some of the accounts, you'd have sworn I had tire tracks on my back. The poor guy just got reamed in the press. He's probably off in a mental institution somewhere. Later I got so many letters saying I would've won the race had it not been for the motorcycle.

Maybe I would have, maybe I wouldn't have. I don't know. But it would have been fun had it not been there, just to see. Because I was flying. At that point, it seemed like for every ten steps Salazar was taking, I was taking twenty. I was closing the gap.

It's like a horse race. The horse that comes from behind, charging ahead with everything he has, the one with the momentum, that's often the horse that wins. I was that horse.

I didn't say that at the time, of course. It would have sounded like I was making excuses and I wasn't. I don't know what would have happened had the motorcycle not been there. Maybe something else would have gone wrong. Who knows?

You couldn't have asked for a more exciting finish, that's for sure. One thing about the 1982 Boston, it's one of the very few athletic contests where people remember who got second place.

These days, if you get second place in the Boston Marathon, you win something like fifty thousand dollars. In 1982, I got a clock.

It's still in my living room, and it's still ticking.

I was talking to the press and my feet were dying. I took

my shoes off and put them on the table in front of me. Coach Squires is a devout Catholic like me, and I promised him the shoes so his church could auction them off in a fundraiser.

After about ninety minutes, I turned around to answer questions from the media behind me. When I turned back to the front after talking to them, my shoes were gone. Mary had already gone back to the room, so I thought, well, she probably has them with her.

After more than two hours, Kevin Ryan, one of the athletic coordinators for New Balance, said, "Dickie, that's enough. You've more than talked to the press. You need to get up to your room." I *was* beat. I'd run twenty-six miles, then sat for two hours. I could hardly move. Not to mention the sunburn. Everything hurt.

I hobbled back to the room in my socks. I was hurting bad. Mary drew me a bath and I stretched out in it, soaking with a Coke. I was in the tub, reflecting on the day, trying to memorize every moment, when the phone rang.

"Is this Dick Beardsley's room?" the guy asked Mary.

"Yes," she said.

"Is he there?"

"Well, he is, but he's in the tub."

"Tell him I'm the guy who took his shoes. Thanks a lot!" Click.

Not only did he have the gall to steal my shoes, he was gloating. As irritated as I was, at least I knew what had happened to them. I wish he would have just asked. I would have given him something. Two little kids at the finish line had asked. One of them wanted my painter's cap and I gave it to him. The other kid wanted my sponge. No problem. I thought I might be naked before too long.

In the tub I wondered what I could have done differently to have changed the outcome of the race. Then I decided, nothing. *Nothing.* I was relaxing in the tub, when this feeling of serenity washed over me. I was completely at peace with the race, with myself, with life. I was happy. It had been so fun, so exciting, and I wouldn't have changed a single thing. What a great story!

The phone rang again. This time it was Sid Hartman, a sportswriter for the Minneapolis *Star Tribune*. "Hi Dick," he said, "what a great race," blah, blah, blah. And then: "How does it feel to be a loser?"

Huh?

I was so stunned by the question I was tempted to say, "Gee, Sid, you should know."

Instead I said, "If that's being a loser, I'll take being a loser every cotton-pickin' time. I just ran the best race of my life!"

Sid doesn't have a lot of time for runners if you look at how much space he devotes to them in his column. But he's always been nice to me. After a minute or so he mellowed out a little and we talked.

Mary and I considered ordering room service, knowing it would be crazy in public. Then I thought, no, the race is over, it's time to give back to the running community. We'd go down to the hotel restaurant, I'd sign autographs, and do the right thing.

Before we left the room, I called each of my folks. Mom was crying: "Oh Dick, I'm so proud of you!" Then I called my dad. He couldn't even talk to me, he was sobbing that hard. He was so emotional. I was too. Eventually I got it out. I told him I was thinking about him before the race, during the race, at the one-mile-to-go point, everything. He didn't say much. He was still sobbing. But I thanked him again for the round-trip ticket to the marathon, the one we'd used to pay Mary's way out there, as it turned out. "I love you, Dad," I said. "I love you, too, D. . . ."

We walked down to the hotel restaurant and were bombarded by people right away. The great thing about marathoning is, I'd run a 2:08-something and someone else had run a 4:08-something, but maybe it was their first race, and maybe they'd worked just as hard for their time as I had for mine. Maybe harder. You bonded. You both survived a marathon, no small feat.

At the restaurant we ran into George Hirsch, at the time the publisher of *The Runner* and later *Runner's World.* George had always been so nice to me and tonight he wanted to buy Mary and me dinner. "Aw George, you don't have to do that," I told him. But he insisted.

The New Balance factory and offices are in Boston. They had a big party that night, which we attended. Everybody was dancing and having a great time. Jim Davis, chairman and CEO of New Balance, got up and the band stopped. He was in tears, and in no time I was, too. He told the crowd, "We've never had a runner like Dick from the standpoint of his ability, but even more from the standpoint of his personality. No matter how much he achieves, he's still a regular guy, talking to people, doing things for kids. . . ."

I thought back to the day I'd crashed that sporting goods convention and how much it had meant when Hal DeWaltoff offered me some encouragement. The Boston Marathon was my way of saying *"Thank you."*

The next morning, the company took the opportunity to say, "You're welcome!" Our phone rang about seven-thirty. It was Jim Davis. "Dick," he said, "there's a white stretch limo waiting for you downstairs. You don't have to hurry, but when you're ready, the limo will take you anywhere you want to go. Anything you want to see in Boston, anything you want to eat, any souvenir you want to buy, it's on New Balance. The only thing I ask is that you come by the office about two-thirty this afternoon."

We took him up on it, of course. We had a wonderful day, seeing the sights and doing the tourist thing. We arrived at New Balance at two-thirty sharp. We walked into the office, which was bustling with people. They saw me and everyone fell silent. Everything stopped. It was weird. Then all of a sud-

South Dakota State University Men's Cross-Country Team, 1978. Back row, left to right: Coach Scott Underwood, Mike Dunlap, Mark Bills, Mike Bills, Ken Cizadlo. Front row, left to right: Joel Brandt, me, Paul Brandt. Photograph courtesy of Don L. Arend.

The London Marathon, March 29, 1981. Inge Simonsen of Norway (right) and I tied for first place at 2:11:48. Photograph copyright Bettman/Corbis.

Grandma's Marathon in Duluth, June 20, 1981. I won the race in 2:09:37, still a course record. Mary is in the chute with me—her hair is flying across her face. Reprinted with permission of the *Duluth News Tribune*. Photograph by Joey McLeister.

The Boston Marathon, April 19, 1982. I had a stride or two on world record holder Alberto Salazar for most of the race, like right here at Coolidge Corner with about two miles to go. *Boston Globe* photograph by John Blanding; reprinted with permission.

At Boston, we were surrounded by police escorts and other officials as we raced toward the finish line. The press bus is in the background. AP/Wide World Photos.

Salazar turned around to check on me just yards from the finish at Boston.
AP/Wide World Photos.

Seconds after the Boston finish, Salazar and I congratulated each other on a great race. AP/Wide World Photos.

Rush City, Minnesota, April 22, 1982, three days after the Boston Marathon. Mary and I acknowledged a standing ovation at the hometown celebration in the high school gym. Staff photograph from *Chisago County Press*; reprinted by permission.

On the farm in Rush City.

The Napa Valley Marathon, March 8, 1987. I won the race in a course record 2:16:20 and qualified for the 1988 Olympic Trials. Photograph by Ken Lee; copyright 2000.

I started my leg of the Olympic Torch Run in Rush City on June 28, 1990.
Photograph courtesy of Mark Morson/*St. Paul Pioneer Press.*

I love giving speeches. This one was to graduate students of the University of Minnesota School of Agriculture in June 1993. Photograph courtesy of *Star Tribune*, 2000.

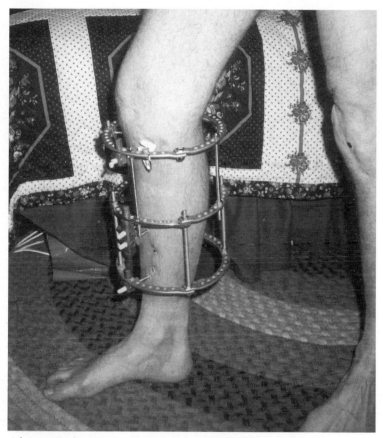

After major knee surgery in October 1995, titanium rods were screwed into the bone, and stainless steel halos kept them in place.

For many years I was WCCO Radio's "Voice of the Twin Cities
Marathon." Here I am interviewing well-known businessman, author, and
running enthusiast Harvey Mackay. Coach Wenmark is in the background.

I love my work as a fishing guide.

The Beardsley family, February 2000.

den, everyone started clapping. I felt like I was in a movie. *Everyone* was clapping. It gave me chills.

I was escorted into Jim Davis's office. "Here Dick," he said. "This is for you. It's just a little thank-you from us." It was a check for five thousand bucks. "Listen," he continued. "We've been working on a contract all morning. . . ."

He had more people he wanted me to talk with. I went into an office where they had a three-year contract all ready for me to sign. Thirty thousand dollars a year. I'd been making twelve thousand.

Thirty thousand dollars a year. To run! This was unbelievable.

But the folks at Adidas had done me a favor in that they got me thinking. I didn't want to jump on anything too quickly. I needed some advice.

"Sign right here," the guy from New Balance said, smiling. They were all being so nice, but still I felt pressured.

"I have to think about this," I said.

"Nah, just sign it," one of them suggested.

I held firm. I thanked them profusely. I'd be in touch.

Mary and I flew into Minneapolis Wednesday night. We got off the plane and there were two or three hundred people in the lobby of the airport, banners up everywhere, all the major news stations. There were even a couple of high school bands on hand. What a homecoming! Eventually we made our way to the car and drove the hour or so back to our cabin near Rush City. We got into town about eleven at night. Nobody there knew when to expect us. They were having a little celebration at the high school the next morning, we'd been told, but we were unprepared for what we saw as we drove through town. It seemed like there was a banner in every window! I was overwhelmed.

By ten o'clock Thursday morning the whole town had closed down. They'd canceled school, closed businesses. Every one of about a thousand people, it seemed, had converged on the high school. People were sitting on top of one another—

you could not fit one more body into that gym. There was a proclamation from the governor and a key to the city. They gave Mary a big bouquet of flowers and put a lei around my neck. The band had only had a couple days to learn the music from the movie *Chariots of Fire*—and you could tell. But I was so touched. I was supposed to be up there saying something, but I couldn't speak for just the longest time. It was difficult to talk without crying.

After it was over, all the kids wanted autographs.

I happily obliged.

I won the Robert E. DeCelle award in 1982, which recognizes the United States's outstanding male distance runner. That was a big honor for me.

Less than two weeks after Boston, my dad quit drinking. He never had another drop, not a drop, for the remaining fourteen years of his life.

CHAPTER 5

A Change of Pace

I NEVER SHOULD HAVE COMMITTED to Grandma's Marathon again. I had no idea how much Boston would take out of me. Not only that, but it would have been fun to just bask in that for a while. I couldn't, though. I had to start training for Grandma's.

For the first time in my career, I didn't look forward to the next race. How could I? How could it possibly compare to the Boston Marathon—and especially to that finish?

I needed a vacation. I needed about a month off from running. Instead I was in Duluth, with everyone talking world record. Everybody except me.

I was starting to see a life beyond marathoning. Mary and I bought a farm northwest of Rush City. It was sixty acres, with an option of additional acres later if we wanted. Most everything was in really good condition, though the barn would have to be remodeled for dairying. Dennis Frandsen helped us with the paperwork. He also helped us get a good deal on some equipment. Beardsley's Marathon Dairy: that's what we were calling it. I'd been dreaming of dairy farming since I was a kid. The current owners wouldn't be moving out until September, so we couldn't move in until then, but I was looking forward to it.

Farming's a tough life. So is marathoning. Lots of hard work, little time off. Each life conditioned me for the other one.

Grandma's Marathon was June 21, 1982. My right hamstring had finally healed, the one that slowed me down so much with a half mile to go at Boston. But it had been tough going. Training was more of an effort, and I wasn't having as much fun.

For the first time in my career, I wasn't excited to race. Not a bit. I really wasn't. Scott Keenan had arranged for me to have a "rabbit" at Grandma's. It was a guy from California who was going to run with me. He was really good at 15Ks and half marathons. He'd take the pace out and break the wind for me, just be there for me for at least fifteen miles.

Four or five miles into the race the guy was already laboring a little bit. No wonder. It was clear and warm, and there was a southerly wind. It was going to be a rough day. At six, seven miles we should have been waltzing along. Instead the wind was picking up and I was breaking it for *him*. I thought, they're paying him for this?

That year they had a new clock, which I loved. Actually there were three clocks on the back of this vehicle. One showed your running time, one gave your projected winning time, and the third gave you your pace per mile.

I was on world record pace for about eight miles, but I couldn't keep it up.

At ten miles, my rabbit dropped out and I was all by myself.

At thirteen miles, that was all I could think about: I'm only half finished! I was depressed. I was depressed even before I got a pebble in the heel of my left shoe. I had the lead, but no lead's big enough until you cross the finish line, and I didn't want to take the time to empty my shoe and lace it again. So I kept running and every time I landed on my left foot the pebble dug into my heel like a knife. I ran that way the entire second half of the marathon.

Coming off Boston, I felt like I was getting crushed under the weight of people's expectations. It was so hot and I was out there by myself bucking the wind. When I won the race in 2:14:49, I was ecstatic, mostly because it was *over*.

Having my dad there made it all worth it. He quit drinking May 1, about the same time he got laid off from his job. Might as well give it the acid test right away, I guess he thought. I was like a lot of other guys in that I had trouble telling Dad just how much I loved him and how proud I was of him. I wanted to change that.

He and my stepmom stayed overnight. The day after the race was Father's Day. Before they left I handed Dad a card and told him not to open it until he got home. That night he called. "D . . ." he said, but he could barely get it out he was bawling so hard. Inside the Father's Day card I'd enclosed a check for five hundred dollars and told him it was pop money.

Dad had quit drinking before, but it felt different this time. Even though he was out of work, he had a resolve I'd never seen before. Maybe it had something to do with my running, maybe it didn't. I knew one thing. Any doubts he had about me in high school were gone. It almost seemed like he was looking up to *me* now.

Every May 1 I called to congratulate him on another year of sobriety, never dreaming I'd face my own challenge with it someday.

Running was enough of a challenge at the moment.

I was just not ready to run another marathon as soon as I did. I was getting burned out. After Boston, New Balance and I had agreed to a three-year contract where I got fifty-five thousand dollars each of the first two years, and seventy thousand the third—not counting bonuses. I should have taken time off after that and given my body a chance to recover.

But no. I ran Grandma's and *still* I didn't let up.

A New Balance rep in Alaska invited me up there a week after the marathon, for what I thought was going to be mostly sightseeing. Wrong. There were all these store appearances, shorter races, and a 10K. The rep said I didn't have to run hard, that people just wanted to see me. I didn't believe him. If you invited Michael Jordan somewhere, people wouldn't want to watch him shoot free throws. They'd want to see him dunk the frickin' basketball.

I'm no Michael Jordan, but back then there were a lot of runners who wanted to be able to say they beat Dick Beardsley in a race.

So I gave them one. I won the 10K in about thirty minutes, on a hilly course.

I got back to Minnesota, more in need of a vacation than ever. I should have taken the rest of the summer off, but the folks from the New York City Marathon had been calling. They wanted me back in October. Ten thousand bucks, they said, just for showing up. Ten thousand dollars! That was a lot of money we could sink into our farm. Plus Salazar was going to be there.

"You don't have anything to prove to Salazar," Coach said. "The next time you ought to face him is at the Olympic Trials. You *do not need* to race in New York this year."

Coach said it, Mary said it, everybody said it. I didn't listen to any of them.

Mary didn't force the issue. When it came to my running, she might give an opinion once in a while, but the minute I disagreed, she backed off. It wasn't that she was completely behind everything I did. She knew I wasn't enjoying the races as much as I'd been before Boston, but she figured, well, let him find out for himself. It kept the peace.

I couldn't admit this for many years, but I was afraid that if I took a break from running I'd lose it. It took me even longer to admit that I was losing it because I wouldn't take a break.

It was my drug of choice.

I went back to Atlanta to train for New York.

It was in Atlanta that everything started to unravel. My Achilles started to bother me. When that happens, it'll be tight when you first wake up in the morning. Then you'll walk around and it loosens up and stops hurting. But pretty soon it stays tight for the whole day. After a while you can actually hear it squeak. Soon after that it starts to get thick and inflamed, you develop little nodules, and it hurts all the time.

My Achilles hurt *constantly.*

Other than that, I was in great shape. The Achilles won't matter, I told myself. Sometimes my knee gave me fits, and then I'd get in a race and wouldn't even feel it. If I ignore my Achilles, I thought, maybe it'll go away.

The New York City Marathon was October 24, 1982.

The day before, I took a taxi out to about the twenty-two-mile mark. I wanted to jog the last four miles of the course, to get really familiar with the route in case it boiled down to a sprint at the end like Boston had. As I ran through Central Park my Achilles hurt so much I could hardly walk, let alone run.

I got back to the hotel, found a garbage can, filled it with ice, and went back to my room. I took some aspirin, stuck my leg in the garbage can, and tried to tell myself it would be fine. It would be fine. Wouldn't it?

The next morning I boarded the special bus they used to escort the elite runners to the starting line. I felt bad because it was so cold and windy, and twenty thousand other people were trying to stay warm with plastic bags.

I started stretching and loosening up in this nice, warm building. Salazar was in one corner and I was in another. I looked over at him once in a while, and I could feel him doing the same to me.

The gun went off and I was in trouble immediately. We were on the Verrazano Narrows Bridge. I could almost feel it bouncing with that many people. By the time I came down off the bridge my left calf was already tight. That wasn't good, because what happened was—even though it was just a little bit—I started favoring one leg. The next thing I knew, my right calf cramped up. There was no spring in my legs. I felt like I was running flat-footed.

There was a big group of us and we were running along at about a five-minute pace. At six miles I was moving all over the road trying to get comfortable, but it was no use. My legs felt like rocks. I was in deep trouble. My legs were cramping up really badly at about eight, ten miles, and I dropped off the pace at about twelve. As I came off the Queensboro Bridge at sixteen miles or so, I was tempted to just drop out. I limped along the rest of the race as best I could, and finished thirtieth at 2:18:12.

I made my way to the press room with Mary. We took seats in the back. Right away a reporter walked up and stuck a microphone in my face, thinking he was going to interview Salazar, the winner. "Alberto . . ." he began. I managed a smile. "I'm not Alberto," I told him. "I'm Dick Beardsley."

A few minutes later they wanted me up front. I said okay, and answered their questions. I didn't try to hide my disappointment, nor did I offer any excuses. But I was crushed, and it was obvious. I hoped the tears would look like sweat from the lights. This was humiliating! Before the race, everybody was talking about Salazar and Beardsley, Salazar and Beardsley. The big rematch. Someone from the New York paper had wanted us to pose with our dukes up, everyone was so excited about this race. Now I felt like the biggest joke.

I excused myself after several minutes and told them, you know, there'll be another race sometime. I walked to the back and couldn't believe what I was hearing from a room full of reporters.

Applause.

My Achilles tendon was shredded. In November, New Balance sent me to Edmonton, Alberta, to see a doctor up there. He put a cast on my leg and I wore it for six weeks before flying back there to have it removed.

It didn't help.

I might need surgery, he said.

By the end of the year I couldn't run at all.

I was determined to stay in shape, somehow. I put thousands of miles on my stationary bike. That wasn't enough, though. Plus it was so boring it drove me crazy.

What was I going to do?

Then I had an idea. I would shovel snow! Lots of snow . . .

I shoveled so much, soon our whole farm had been dug out, and I started rearranging snow. After a while I had to stay pretty much behind our barn because otherwise the neighbors would have thought I *had* gone crazy.

I'd started using this hypoxic simulator while I shoveled. I had a mask strapped to my face and a couple of canisters harnessed to my shoulders. I was simulating training at high altitudes.

I patterned a week of shoveling with the simulator the same way I used to design a week of runs. Sunday instead of a two-and-a-half-hour run, I did two and a half hours of steady shoveling. Monday I recovered a little bit, shoveling at an easy pace for forty-five minutes to an hour. Tuesday instead of repeat miles I did repeat shoveling. I did my warm-up shovel, followed by what I called fartlek shoveling. I shoveled as hard as I could for two minutes, backed off for one minute, shoveled as hard as I could for two minutes, and so on—for ninety minutes or so. Wednesday was my medium tempo shovel, again for about ninety minutes. Thursday's workout was similar to Tuesday's. Friday I took it kind of easy, shoveling for thirty to forty-five minutes. Saturday was race day. I shoveled as hard and as fast as I would have if I was racing, and I didn't let up.

Shoveling's hard work to begin with. Try it with a hypoxic simulator sometime. You'll understand why even though I wasn't marathoning, I was probably in the best shape of my life. My upper body had never been this strong.

I slowly, slowly got back into my running and after a few months of very tentative training I thought, well, maybe I can try a race. Eight miles into the Manufacturers Hanover Brooklyn Half Marathon in March of 1983, my Achilles was shot again. They put me in a cast again. I had surgery in late July that year. The doctors warned me not to train for six months, but the Olympic review board wouldn't give me a bye into the following year's Trials. I was determined to keep training for them and started in again after only six weeks.

I ruined the tendon once more. This time, they told me, my running career was over. My bid for the 1984 Olympic team certainly was.

I didn't give up.

In a desperate attempt to qualify for the trials, I ran the Los Angeles Marathon in February of 1984.

I had to drop out at seven miles because the Achilles hurt so badly.

Two days later I had more surgery on it.

It took several months, but finally I decided my competitive running days might be over. I might have messed myself up beyond repair. I couldn't face the emptiness that brought on, so I threw myself into our dairy farm. Mary and I were very active in the community. We were still hoping for a family, although it was getting harder to stay upbeat about that, too. Still, farming didn't allow much time for feeling sorry for yourself, and I wasn't one to do that anyway. I was going to make the best of life, whatever it handed me. I planted a crop that spring, we were baling hay that summer, and I had heifers I could start breeding soon. A contractor was renovating the barn, inside and out.

It was exciting, but it wasn't racing.

In late summer the folks from the Twin Cities Marathon were on the phone. Wouldn't that be something, I thought, if a Minnesota boy could win the two greatest marathons here?

Sure, I said. I'll run Twin Cities.

The race was September 30, 1984. I was in the lead pack for the first five or six miles, running a five-minute pace. But I was hurting and I couldn't hold it. A marathon's not something you can fake. I was in good shape, but it wasn't marathon shape. I finished in forty-fifth place, at 2:30:05. There was a big hand as I came in, which I appreciated.

Usually at Twin Cities I was sitting in the back of a truck, doing the play-by-play broadcast for WCCO Radio. That was *almost* as much fun as running. I loved it.

Before I ran that marathon, the people associated with the Beijing International Marathon in China stepped up the pressure to get me over there. The race was October 14, 1984— two weeks after Twin Cities.

It had never worked out with my schedule, and that year would be no exception. I kept telling them, "Nah, I can't. I just ran a marathon, I'm having problems with my Achilles, and I'm not in very good shape." We don't care, they said, we just want you to come and race. "But I'm hitting a busy time on the farm," I continued to object. We were about to start milking and there was no one to cover for us.

What would it take to get me there, they wanted to know. I thought about it for a minute, then proposed something so outlandish—at least at that stage of my career—I knew they'd turn me down. "Okay," I said. "You'd have to bring Mary over there with me and pay me fifteen thousand dollars."

Fine, they said.

"Mary!" I told her. "They don't care how fast I run. They're going to pay us fifteen thousand dollars! We can buy a dozen bred heifers with that kind of money!"

It was the first time I ran strictly for the cash.

They put us up in what was one of their fancier hotels. Mary woke me up in the middle of our first night there. "Dick! Dick! What's that noise?" I turned on the light, we looked up at the screen covering some ductwork in the ceiling, and there were these huge *rats* walking back and forth across this grate. Big honkin' hairy rats. I could forget about getting much sleep this trip.

I went out in the morning for a run through a park and could not believe the number of people out exercising! It was 5:00 A.M. and it seemed like the whole city was out for a jog or a walk. There was an old man doing what looked like splits, except he was standing up. His one leg was straight up alongside the trunk of this tree. It was amazing to me how excited *everyone* seemed about fitness.

Race day came and I went out at about a six-minute pace. Not fast enough to win, of course, but a respectable clip. Temperatures were in the upper seventies, which for a marathon is brutal. The first thing I noticed was, as enthusiastic as everybody was about running, no one cheered us on the course. I wondered if maybe there was a rule against it.

The first time I came upon an aid station, I got something to drink. Whatever it was upset my stomach and I didn't drink the rest of the way in. Talk about suicide! Twenty-six miles on a hot day and no water! This was *not* going to be good. To my amazement, I got to the twenty-mile mark in exactly two hours. Six-minute pace.

I started losing it immediately, though. I was dehydrated. I wanted to quit. Oh, I wanted to quit! But the race promoters wanted one thing in exchange for the trip and the money. They wanted me to finish, no matter what. "You're a 2:08 marathoner," they said when we set this thing up. "We just want you to run. We don't care how you finish. We just want you to finish the race."

I promised them I'd finish.

It took me fifty-six minutes to go the last ten kilometers, 6.2 miles. I collapsed as I crossed the finish line. I was dehydrated and incoherent.

Right away they took me to the medical tent for an IV. Who knows what's in *that,* I thought, but I started feeling better immediately. By that night I felt fine. They had a huge banquet, which the vice president of China attended.

To show us their hospitality, they served a delicacy called thousand-year-old eggs. They took hard-boiled eggs, immersed them in pig's urine, and buried them in the ground for thirty days. Then they brought them up, washed them off, placed them in fancy bowls, and set them on the table in front of us.

When they passed them around, you did not say no. When they passed the sake, you were expected to partake. When they passed the thousand-year-old eggs, you were expected to partake. I partook of an egg and honest to God I thought I was going to hurl all over their fancy bowls. It was awful. They were eating them like peanut M&Ms and I couldn't watch.

Mary and I were homesick. We were twenty miles from the Great Wall and had been looking forward to seeing it. But between the rats and the race and now the thousand-year-old eggs, we decided we'd had enough sightseeing for one lifetime.

My life beyond running was marching forward. It was time to get back to it.

By 1986 we had one of the top dairy herds in Minnesota.

In January of that year we adopted our son, Andy, battling a harrowing amount of red tape, paperwork, and uncertainty. I had made two trips to Honduras and had gotten robbed at gunpoint in El Salvador. But finally, finally we had our son.

It wasn't long before I started fantasizing that my retirement and rest had allowed my Achilles injury to heal. The fantasies grew stronger with each run. In May of 1986 I saw Bill Wenmark at the Syttende Mai race in Grantsburg, Wisconsin. I was just making an appearance there, not running. Bill and I got to talking and I thought, man, I have to go for it. I had to try for the Olympics in 1988.

I knew Bill from the American Lung Association Marathon Training Program—he was the director. We talked about the possibility of him becoming my coach. He said he'd think about it. Bill owned a chain of urgent care centers and coached a lot of marathoners, though most of them were beginners.

Mary and I had the talk. She knew one thing: she didn't want to live with someone who couldn't live with himself, which is what would happen if I didn't give this a shot.

We sold the farm in June 1986 and got ready to move back to the Twin Cities, where I'd start my bid for a comeback. The goal was to qualify for the Olympic team, at the Trials in May 1988.

As anxious as I was to get back into some serious training, it hurt to leave the farm. After the auction, after everyone had been by to pick up what they'd bought, I walked into the barn. It was eerie it was so quiet. It was just me and a little bit of a breeze. No cows bellerin', nothing. I climbed up in the hayloft and had a seat on a broken bale.

I sighed.

I didn't have a choice. I had to go for this. It hurt so much to miss the Trials in 1984. If I waited until 1992 I'd be too old. My only chance was 1988.

It was my only chance, and I had to take it. I refused to be milking cows at age seventy-five, wondering what *if*. I'd never be able to forgive myself. Failing was one thing. Not giving it my best was not an option.

Still, it hurt to leave. I was making a fair amount of money when we bought this place, and we'd sunk piles into it. Between the money and the sweat, it was really a showcase. I was proud of it. Goodbyes *suck*, even if it was just a stupid old barn.

We rented a house in the Minneapolis suburb of Plymouth in September 1986. Mary started working for a woman who had her own business cleaning houses. She liked it. One thing about dairy farming, it made most other jobs seem easy.

I took care of Andy when I wasn't training. On a typical day I got up early so I could run before Mary went to work. Then I worked out on the treadmill in the morning and watched Andy. I did my outdoor workout in the afternoon when Mary got home.

We were scraping by, but oh, just barely. I made some money doing clinics and speaking, but it didn't amount to much. At the peak of my speaking career, right after Boston, I could do three or four talks a month and make thirty thousand a year. Once I got injured, my stock went down pretty quickly. I was still in demand as a speaker, but not so much for the high-paying, high-profile engagements.

Bill Wenmark took a scientific approach to my training. He had a team of people working with me: a massage therapist, a chiropractor, some doctors.

I hadn't been competing seriously for a few years and I was a different runner. I looked at my old logbooks, the ones I recorded my workouts in, and wondered who that person was. The workouts were a lot more effort now. Five or ten years before, I could go out and hammer myself five days in a row and be fine. When I started working with Wenmark it was clear I couldn't do the brutal track workouts without taking an extra day or two of easy runs in between. That bothered me a lot, but Bill was good about keeping me motivated.

That's why I didn't go back and seek Squires's help this time. Squires was great and I loved him, but I needed someone who could be out on the track with me at times, monitoring me and keeping my spirits up.

I was training full time, seven days a week, two workouts a day. I put in an average of a hundred miles a week, but I also swam, lifted weights, biked, and whatever else the experts told me to do.

In January 1987 I won the St. Paul Winter Carnival Half Marathon, setting a course record in 1:07:20.

Bill and I decided the Napa Valley Marathon would be my comeback race. The one where I qualified for the Olympic Trials. It was a beautiful course. The weather was usually great for racing. There wouldn't be a crush of media there, either. Who needed the extra pressure? I felt enough pressure as it was.

The race was March 8, 1987. My goal was to run a sub 2:20. That would get me into the Trials.

From the first mile on, I was by myself. I passed the halfway point in 1:07:10 and felt great. We were having light showers, it was in the low forties, and I was feeling really, really good.

I continued to feel great—as great as you can feel in a marathon—until about mile twenty-three. It was at that point I got one of the worst cramps of my life. We were running on a highway and for the first ten miles we could run on either side of the road. I ran right down the middle. Later on in the race we had to run on the right side of the highway. Because of the way the road dipped, I put more strain on my right calf than my left and it was cramping up really badly.

The last three miles, I was once again in the position of not knowing if I could finish the race.

That's what makes marathoning so suspenseful. You never know what's going to go wrong or when. Maybe it's a side ache, maybe it's a cramp, maybe you get dehydrated. I don't remember a race where everything went right. Things were not going right in Napa.

There was so much riding on things going right! Financially, selling the farm had been a huge mistake. Our move to the Cities so I could train for the Trials was a disaster if you looked at our bank account. We had nothing. We were wiped out.

I wasn't looking at it that way, of course. But it wasn't just me we were talking about.

I wanted a qualifying time *so badly,* if only to prove I hadn't been irresponsible in uprooting my family again so I could chase that pot of Olympic gold.

I was going to run a sub 2:20 if it killed me.

Through sheer force of will, I crossed the finish line in first place. In 2:16:20! I'd earned a spot at the Trials! I collapsed in Coach's arms. Maybe this had been the right thing to do after all.

My time at Napa is still a course record.

In June 1987 I made a return trip to Grandma's and struggled the entire race. I couldn't get into my rhythm. As I crossed the Lester River at about the eighteen-mile mark, I couldn't even see the leader. An elderly gentleman watching the race hollered, "*Beardsley!* You're all washed up!" I didn't get mad, but I made eye contact. "I'm doing the best I can today" was all I offered.

I came in fifteenth at 2:22:28.

Bill and I pressed on. In December that year I got a sponsor, Creamettes, which thrilled me. They make pasta, a natural for runners to promote. There was a little money coming in now, maybe a thousand dollars a month, something like that.

Wenmark didn't have the same athlete to coach that Squires did. My body was wearing out. The longest I was injury-free now was about four months. It was always something. I was always in recovery. I may as well have been held together with duct tape.

I continued to have problems with my knee and my Achilles. Now my calves were going and required surgery. When you start exercising, your calf muscles expand and the lining that covers them is supposed to expand with them. For some reason mine wasn't. When I ran, the muscles expanded but the lining didn't . . . and oh, the pain was unbelievable.

I hoped to somehow be in shape for the Trials, set for April 24, 1988.

This was it. The Olympic Trials. We started in a grassy field near Hoboken, New Jersey. Behind us was the Statue of Liberty and talk about an awesome sight! Breathtaking.

The race began. We hit the first mile in about five minutes and right away I thought, oh, this is not good. I felt like I was working way too hard. I'd felt that way early in other races before, though, and tried not to let it bother me.

We got to two, three miles and already I was starting to drop off the pace. At about five miles some guys I knew tapped me on the shoulder and said, "Come on Dickie, come with us. Suck in behind us, we'll pull you along."

But I couldn't. I just couldn't. I don't know why. I felt like the soles of my shoes and the pavement beneath them were made of Velcro—every step was that much of an effort. If I didn't start feeling better soon, two and a half years of training would have been for nothing. Selling the farm, moving my family again, all of it—for nothing.

I wasn't giving up.

I wasn't giving up, but reality was starting to sink in. By about the halfway point I couldn't see the lead pack anymore. Unless the earth opened up and swallowed everyone in front of me, I wasn't going to make the Olympic team.

I kept running, and after a while I heard—on the radios some spectators had—who the top three finishers were.

"These three runners have earned a spot on the U.S. Olympic team . . ." I heard an announcer say.

I crossed the finish line in 2:27:21. Forty-fifth place.

Well, that was it.

My competitive running days were over.

But you know what? I was relieved. I was happy! I'd felt like dropping out of the race, but I hadn't. I'd hung in there, and I was proud of that.

I was also very proud that I'd taken one more shot at the Olympics. That would have been a regret I couldn't have lived with, not trying.

I'd tried.

Now it was time to retire.

Mary and I celebrated in New York City.

I didn't really have a plan for myself after the Trials, but I started looking for a job right away. My contract with Creamettes wasn't up yet, and I had an offer from them to sell pasta to grocery stores. I couldn't see myself doing that, though. Eventually I got a job with Land O'Lakes as a nutritionist and feed sales representative in Volga, South Dakota. I started in September, and moved the family once again.

I didn't mind the work. I was out in the country consulting with different farmers every day. I missed farming so much I'd tell them, you know, if you ever want a break from milking cows, let me know, I'll come over. And I did. Mary even came with me a few times.

We couldn't buy another farm because we were broke. Not that Mary wanted to. Her enthusiasm for farming was waning. It's a hard life. It would have to be a perfect situation, she told me, before I should even bother bringing it up again. I still had dreams of owning another farm, but for the most part I kept those to myself.

If I couldn't farm I wanted to be a fishing guide. But that's a tough way to make a living, too, and I had a family to support.

Mary liked it in Volga. She liked my steady paycheck with Land O'Lakes. She liked the good benefits and the company car. It was such a relief for her after all the uncertainty when I was training. She had her own housecleaning business now, and liked being closer to her parents. Mary never complained about moving around a lot, but this time, I got the definite impression she wanted to stay put.

I kept running. Now it was strictly for fun. I'd always wanted to do a fifty-mile race, sometimes called an ultra marathon. That sounded fun.

In July 1988 I ran the Minnesota Voyageur Trail Ultra, which went from Carlton, Minnesota, to Duluth—and back. It was all on wilderness trails and I was excited.

A few hundred people were there, and I started with the lead pack. I had no idea what awaited me, and no respect for the distance. After about three miles it still felt like we were walking, so I took off. I got a big lead.

This wasn't like a marathon course. Again, it was on trails, and part of it was so steep we had to hold onto tree roots to keep going.

At about fifteen miles I came down a hill, hit a tree root, and went flying. I wondered if I'd broken my ankle. I kept running toward the first-aid tent, about a quarter mile away. They looked at my ankle and suggested I call it a day. No way, I told them. They taped me up.

I got to the halfway point, twenty-five miles, in three hours and twenty minutes. It was time to turn around. I continued to run about a seven-minute pace as the course allowed, while the rest of the leaders were running about an eight- or nine-minute pace.

It took me six hours and twenty-eight minutes to come back. No kidding! More than twice as long to run the second half of the race as the first. I finished the fifty miles in 9:48, placing thirteenth. I wouldn't have finished at all if it weren't for a man named Brian from Duluth. We ran side by side the last twenty miles and took turns convincing each other to hang in. I saw Mary at the finish line and hollered, "If I ever suggest doing anything like this again, will you do me a favor? Will you hit me over the head with a *hammer?*"

I was in the hurt bag. It was the middle of the summer and *hot*. Fifty miles are much, much harder than two marathons. At least with two marathons you'd rest in between. This was like finishing one marathon and starting the next one as soon as you reached the finish line.

For someone less inclined to beat himself silly, that might have posed a problem. But for me, that wasn't the big problem. The big problem was my ankle.

I took the tape off my ankle and it puffed up like a balloon being filled with helium. More first aid. I had a broken ankle! I'd just run *thirty-five miles* on a *broken ankle!*

I thought back to the aid station where they'd first examined it. "Tape 'er up good, boys," I'd said. Apparently they'd listened.

I got to the hospital, where they put a cast on my leg.

I was about to get really familiar with hospitals.

I knew Mary didn't want to leave South Dakota and my first steady paycheck since we'd met, but I couldn't resist looking at the "Farms for Sale" ads in *Hoard's Dairyman*. I talked Mary into looking at a farm in Shafer, Minnesota, during the summer of 1989. She seemed pleased the place was a nightmare: end of story, she thought. It was in such bad shape even I agreed, no way. We were on a trip to see my dad in Michigan, and on the way back the guy who owned the farm talked us—well, me—into coming back for another look. He did his sales pitch and told me how great it could look with just a little fixing up here and there. He talked me into it.

I wasn't going to be able to talk Mary into it, the way it looked. She didn't want to move, she didn't want to start farming again, and even if she did change her mind about moving or farming, she didn't want to move *there*. A lot of guys might think, well, that had better be that. You know, if mama ain't happy . . . But Mary wasn't like that. I knew if we moved despite her objections, I would not be punished. She wouldn't make it hard on me. That's one of the things that's made it easy to stay in love with her all these years. She's a good kid.

I wasn't, though—not in this case. I twisted her arm, I overruled her, and we prepared to move. I put in my notice at Land O'Lakes and Mary told her clients. We moved in September 1989, but she wasn't excited about it—and it showed.

I thought, well, she'll like it once we get settled.

I was wrong.

CHAPTER 6

An Accident Happening

MENTION "POWER TAKEOFF ACCIDENT" to anyone who's been around a farm very long and the first thing they probably think of is death. At least dismemberment, but probably death. A slow, painful, bone-crushing death.

That's what I was having a brush with the morning of Monday, November 13, 1989.

I got up like I did every day, about a quarter to four. I walked out to the barn and went about my business. Except today I had a zillion things to do. Sunday we hadn't done much except milk cows, but Saturday we'd picked corn all day. A neighbor was coming over as soon as the milking was done to help pick more corn. I had three wagon loads to put into the corncrib before that, and I didn't want to keep this guy waiting. Plus they were predicting a snowstorm—a big one—so everything this morning was rush, rush, rush.

I milked the cows, going about a hundred miles an hour.

I skipped breakfast.

I skipped my run.

I even skipped my usual ritual of going inside to say good morning to Mary and Andy. It would have taken too much time.

I was unloading corn and Mary—who by now had taken

Andy to the bus stop and was bedding cows—told me we were out of straw. I yelled at her to keep unloading corn, to keep it going up the elevator. I jumped in the pickup and within minutes was back with more straw. I got out of the truck and the tractor wasn't running. The elevator, which ran off the tractor's power takeoff, was of course not running. Nothing was running.

I started yelling again. Unusual for me, but there was so much to do. "Mary!" I hollered. "What's going on? We have to get this corn unloaded!"

She said the tractor must have run out of gas, it just quit.

Without thinking, I ran, *ran* to the shed, grabbed a six-gallon can, filled it with gas, ran back, jumped on the tractor, and poured the gas in. I jumped down off the tractor, and put the can on the ground.

Now normally I'd jump back in the tractor, sit in the seat, and push in the clutch. I'd make sure the engine was throttled down, the power takeoff lever disengaged. Always. I always did that.

Not this morning, though. It would have taken too much time.

I stood up on the back of the drawbar, which is almost like a bumper on a tractor. There was ice on it, and it was slippery. As I reached up to turn on the ignition, my right leg was off the ground and my left leg was bearing all my weight.

I hit the key, and everything started! Full throttle! Suddenly I was being beaten into the ground. It felt like someone had come up from behind me, grabbed me by the shoulders, and *thrown* me down on the ground as hard as they could. This thing was just eating up my left leg! It was wrapping my leg around the shaft, like wrapping a piece of string around a finger.

My God! *I was caught in the power takeoff!*

My leg got wrapped around to the point where there was hardly anything left of it, and then my whole body started going around and around. The first thing I thought of was these two friends of mine. One had been killed, the other's wife killed, in accidents like this. *I might die out here!*

That wasn't so scary. The scary part was I might never see Mary or Andy again. And this morning I'd been too busy to even say good morning to them. Not only that, I'd been yelling at Mary.

Then I thought, Dick, you idiot! This would *not* have happened if you would have done things the right way. The machine was beating me up, and I was beating myself up.

I screamed for help. Each time I came around, this thing just smacked me into the frozen ground. My head was getting hammered like a rag doll. I thought, man, if I can't get this turned off . . . Mary was probably in the barn, the fans were running, machines going, cows bellering. She'd never hear me.

Each time I came around I reached for the shutoff lever and tried to grab it. Each time I was a foot, a foot and a half short. My arm wasn't long enough.

I started losing consciousness. I knew if that happened, that would be it. I wouldn't be able to fight the machine, and my body would just keep spinning around and around until there was nothing left of it.

I couldn't focus. I couldn't think straight. It felt like everything was in slow motion. Inside my head, things got quiet. It got really bright. It was a cloudy day, spittin' snow, but all I saw was a bright, bright light. I thought, this is kind of neat. For a moment, I wasn't afraid. I was in a different world.

Every time I came around I thought, if I don't get my fingers around this shaft, I'm finished. Things were still in slow motion, but now it was as if my arm had grown a foot, a foot and a half, because—suddenly—I could see the tips of my fingers around this lever!

They were slowly starting to slide off, though. I thought, man, my fingers are sliding off! If I lose the grip this time, that's *it*. Desperate, I flipped the handle as best I could.

Suddenly, everything stopped.

The calm and the quiet and the bright light gave way to deafening noise again. Somehow I got myself unwrapped from the machinery. To this day I can't remember how. My head felt like a huge pumpkin that had been smashed into the ground.

I was *standing* next to the power takeoff, but had no idea how that happened. How did I get free of everything? I'm standing, I thought, so I can't be hurt too badly.

Wrong.

The minute I tried to take a step, my left leg collapsed. My foot was just about in my left ear. Nobody's that flexible. This was the first time I realized I must be in rough shape.

I was lying on the ground thinking, this is not good. I looked down, my coveralls were all ripped off, there was blood everywhere, and I couldn't breathe. That was scary, not being able to take a deep breath. I knew I had to get help. I hurt bad, but I couldn't just lie there. I belly crawled through the mud and the dirt and the snow and the gravel, trying to get to the house. I was shaking, maybe going into shock. I couldn't yell anymore. I just couldn't. I heard the barn door slam and tried to make some sort of noise. I was able to lift my head slightly. Mary was coming toward me, but it looked like there were five of her because I couldn't focus.

"My God Dick! What happened?" she screamed.

"I got caught in the power takeoff! Call 911!"

She ran into the house, called, answered questions. She ran back out to me. I was still where she found me, about a hundred feet from any machinery. To my disbelief, she cried, "Dick! They want to know if you're still caught in the power takeoff!"

I knew then I would survive, because I thought her question was hilarious. I mean, I was terrified, but I could see the humor in this, too. "Mary!" I yelled. *"Look at me! Does it look like I'm still caught in the PTO? No!!"*

Mary must have been in shock. That's what an accident

like this can do. Almost as if to prove it, she ran back into the house and told 911, yes, he *is* still caught in the PTO.

She ran back out and threw some blankets and coats on top of me. It was cold and I was shaking violently. She had this really terrible look on her face and from that I realized how bad off I was. Soon I could hear sirens and thought, this must be the ambulance.

It wasn't. It was the sheriff. The ambulance, I would learn, was lost.

The sheriff—unbelievably—started cracking jokes. Maybe he was terrified, too, and could think of no better way to take my mind off things. Still, I wasn't in the mood.

The ambulance arrived twenty minutes later. It should have taken half that long, at most. If getting lost wasn't enough, they were asking each other what to do: "We've never had a farm accident before!" We lived in a rural community and there were farms everywhere. There was a piece of steel sticking out of my chest—where *that* came from was anyone's guess—and I was thinking, *"Do something!"*

They tried to straighten my leg out and it sent me into hysterics, it hurt that much. The sheriff had to help hold me down. They got this plastic air splint or something on my leg, put my neck in a brace, loaded me into the ambulance, and took off. We were flying.

We got to the hospital, where they catheterized me. I screamed. There are no words to describe the pain.

They did X rays, CAT scans, all kinds of tests. Finally I was given some pain medication, and for two and a half days I was in a fog, I was that doped up.

Turns out I had a punctured lung from broken ribs, a broken right wrist, contusions to my head, and a concussion. I also had a couple of busted vertebrae in my back—but they didn't discover them for five years! I had back problems from this point forward, but the cause took that long to discover.

Then there was the leg. I was surprised I had a leg at all.

The time in the local hospital was just to stabilize me. Then they took me by ambulance to Fairview Southdale Hospital in the Twin Cities. On the way we stopped at a clinic in suburban Minneapolis for an MRI. When they wheeled me in, there were TV lights everywhere and reporters asking— oh, who knows—I was so doped up.

Dr. Richard Schmidt, my orthopedic surgeon, was waiting for me at the hospital. He'd operated on my legs after running injuries and knew me really well. "Dick," he said, "Obviously you need surgery, but we have to wait a few days. There's too much swelling and we need to get you on antibiotics. My biggest concern is infection." He said he didn't know if I'd be able to walk again without a cane or a brace, adding that I could pretty much count on not being able to run again.

I didn't really believe that, though running was the last thing on my mind at the moment. There was too much to worry about with Mary on the farm by herself. But there was no doubt in my mind I'd walk again.

I was in my own room at the hospital, and with the kind of injuries I had they tried to keep me somewhat comfortable with drugs. Otherwise the pain could have sent me back into shock. My broken ribs continued to make breathing difficult, but I tried to oblige the reporters who wanted interviews. When I look at tapes it's obvious I was feeling good from the drugs.

Finally, Friday, Dr. Schmidt said they could operate the next day. He and Bill Simonet would be doing the surgery. Simonet was the orthopedic surgeon for the Minnesota North Stars—this was before they moved to Dallas. Schmidt said he didn't know how it would go, or what would happen, but he'd do his best. He said infection was still a concern. They were going to operate mainly on my left knee, because that's what had been torn apart. All the tendons had been pulled off the bones.

I was not asleep, completely, when surgery started. I heard

the doctor lift my leg and say, "Boy, it's not supposed to do that!" Pause. "The knee shouldn't bend sideways."

The operation took six hours, and no one had promised me I'd still have a leg when it was over.

Afterward, I was afraid to open my eyes.

It felt like I was moving. I looked to see that, yes, I still had my leg! But it was rotating on a machine, like I was pedaling half a bicycle. It hurt. Oh, it hurt. I woke up in post-op, and already they had me in rehab.

The first week in the hospital after surgery was miserable. They gave me enough medication to take the edge off the pain, but that was it. And that darned machine, twenty-four hours a day. The day after the operation they told me, "Richard, we're going to try to get you up." "Whatever you say," I groaned. My ribs were still so sore. So was my arm. Everything hurt *so much*. I was shaking by the time they stood me up, having not been out of bed for days. Now all the blood ran down to the area around my knee and, honest to God, I thought I'd pass out from the pain. I wasn't standing more than twenty seconds when they let me lie down again.

But twenty seconds is fine, they said. That's good, Richard, that's good. It was a start. It was such a relief to get back into bed, just to get my leg elevated again. Except now they had me back on that darned machine.

I was in so much pain I never felt hungry, never wanted to eat. The nurses were on me to eat. "You have to eat, Richard," they kept telling me. "That's the only way you'll heal."

The doctors thought the operation went really well: "As good as could be expected." They said they didn't know what to expect as far as recovery, whether I'd ever walk on my own again. "But you can probably forget about running," they agreed.

You don't know me, I thought.

At night I had terrible nightmares. Always, always I saw the power takeoff, except now it was Mary or Andy caught in it. I'd wake up from the nightmares sweating so much my bedclothes would be soaked. There were many nights when a nurse sat next to my bed, holding my hand until I fell asleep.

The media never let up the entire time I was in the hospital. Not only didn't it bother me, it kind of broke the monotony of being there so long. There was one woman at the hospital switchboard who was pretty much answering calls just for me. The cards, the flowers, the outpouring—it was incredible. Sometimes people got a little protective of me, trying to make sure I got enough rest given the number of phone calls, visitors, and interview requests. So much so this retired farmer from Hutchinson, Minnesota, had to sneak into my room one night just to talk to me. He was having a knee replacement and we had a nice chat. Every day after that he came in to talk, until they let him go home.

But always, always, it was this darned machine. It hurt so much, and it was going all the time. I had no reprieve from it and oh, the pain. . . .

The overnight nurse was really nice. She'd come in when I couldn't sleep and we'd talk. One night I asked her, do you think you could turn this machine off for like, half an hour? She said no, she could get in trouble for doing that.

I asked and asked, and she always said, no, we can't do that.

I begged her.

Finally after about a week she said she'd shut it off for an hour. To have my leg out of that thing and let it be still for a whole *hour*—I can't tell you how good that felt! It felt so much better than any pain medicine. It just felt *so good*.

Every night she was on duty after that, she'd come in and turn the thing off for an hour.

Each day I started feeling a little better. After about two weeks my ribs weren't as sore, it didn't hurt as much to take deep breaths, and I was getting out of bed more. They started doing more rehab, having me do leg lifts, learning how to walk with crutches, things like that.

After a few weeks the doctor wanted to send me home and let me try recuperating there. I was all for it.

My sister and her husband came to get me since Mary was so busy running the farm. When we arrived at home, they carried me into the house. In the living room was a beautiful recliner that Mary's mom and dad had bought for me. We'd never had a recliner before.

Mary's folks had been there since the accident, helping her. So had her brothers and my dad. The neighbors were wonderful, too. They had shown up the evening of the accident to milk and they were there the next day with four or five corn pickers going through the fields. It was awesome how they helped, held benefits to raise money, and did everything else they could think of.

But keeping everything together was still on Mary's shoulders.

We'd only been in Shafer, in east-central Minnesota, a few months. Longer than I thought it would take for Mary to come around and like being here. She wasn't coming around. And that was before the accident.

Now she was not only stuck here, but she was in charge of everything and working herself silly. She did *not* want to be here, and now I was laid up and couldn't do anything. Not only did she have me to worry about, but there was Andy, too. There was a barn full of cows that required constant attention, on and on and on.

That was my biggest nightmare.

Mary was angry. She was angry that carelessness had caused the accident. She was angry at having to do everything with no help from me. It's worse having me home, she said. Before it was just Andy and the cows and the house and the laundry and the constant phone calls. Now she had to take care of me, too. There wasn't much I could do for myself at first. At least when I was in the hospital she didn't have me to worry about.

Mary continually told me how unhappy she was. She

didn't like being here, I made her come here, thanks for nothing. She was depressed, clinically depressed we later found out, and it was the start of five years of depression.

The farm accident didn't dampen my enthusiasm for life, believe it or not, but it put a huge strain on our marriage. It wasn't easy working this one out.

I had never thought of myself as a selfish person until now. Now I realized I was very selfish in some ways. Like by dragging Mary here to begin with. We'd been married ten years and it suddenly dawned on me we'd *always* done what I wanted. Always, always. Suddenly I realized I wasn't the only person who had needs. I had to start thinking about Mary.

That was the toughest thing to accept about the accident. Not my pain, but the pain I was inflicting on my family. It seemed like Mary and Andy were suffering more than me, and to have caused that—well, it was difficult to live with.

But I also knew it was up to me to stay as upbeat as I could or we'd be in deeper trouble. So I lived for today. I thought, yeah, this is a terrible thing but as the cliché goes, it could have been worse. Yeah, the Beardsleys are going through some tough times, but so are other people. I tried not to think the world was crapping on me. It craps on a lot of people.

Sometimes it wasn't easy to stay upbeat. Like when I found out our health insurance wasn't going to cover any of this.

A few days before the accident, our insurance agent called to say they'd approved our health policy. My insurance from Land O'Lakes had run out October 31, and I assumed the new policy took effect right away.

We got this letter from the insurance company saying, Dick, sorry about your farm accident . . . but by the way, your policy doesn't go into effect until December 1.

I was home recuperating by the time we got around to opening that letter. The mail was hard to keep up with. I thought, well, at least I've had surgery and they can't undo that. Surviving the accident had been the tough part. Anything else life throws me, I thought, will not compare. I didn't worry about the money too much. I was so thankful to be alive and knew the good Lord would provide.

What really helped was having Mary's mom and dad around. They're two of the neatest people I've ever met in my life and we wouldn't have been able to keep going without them. Mary's dad was out doing chores even though he was in his mid-seventies. Sylvia worked constantly, too, cleaning the house and cooking and taking care of Andy.

Now that I was home, I was supposed to continue the leg lifts. Six leg lifts four times a day, the doctor said. That may not sound like much, but at this point it was such a project to lift the leg *once*. It was so much work! It hurt *so much*.

I was in so much pain, and the meds didn't seem to help. I discovered that if I did more than the recommended number of leg lifts, it was almost like those natural endorphins kicked in. I felt better in a way. It hurt to do them, but it almost felt good, too. The first ten days I was home I literally couldn't sleep the pain was so bad. I did more leg lifts since I was awake anyway.

The doctor told me to do four sets of six to ten lifts every day. I did four to eight hundred lifts *every night*.

Hundreds, almost a thousand, leg lifts.

Every night.

Leg up. To the side. Now, on my belly.

On and on and on.

I'd been home less than two weeks, and one morning when I woke up I felt like I was getting the flu. Andy had been sick, and it was going around. My temperature was about a hundred degrees.

Ten o'clock. My temp was 101°, 102°, something like that.

Noon. My temp was 103°. I called the hospital to tell my physical therapist—who came out three times a week—she could skip it this time. She asked a few questions and said she'd be right over. By the time she arrived I was up to 104°. I was so sick I couldn't lift my head off the pillow. She rolled me over, took my brace off, undid the wrap, and the whole top part of my knee was split wide open. The bone was showing and there was orange, yellow, and greenish pus running out of my leg. Almost before she could take all this in she called the hospital, then called my doctor in the Cities. He wanted me down there *now*. Mary had chores, so a retired farmer who lived nearby loaded me into the backseat of his car for the ninety-minute trip.

They put me in a wheelchair to go into the clinic. Once inside, my doctor was finishing up with another patient, but I was so sick I got out of the wheelchair and practically collapsed on the floor. I almost wanted to die, it hurt that much.

They came and got me and put me on a table. The nurse started taking off the wrap, looked at it for a second and quickly covered it back up. The doctor came in. I'll never forget lying there on the table, hallucinating from the pain. The doctor lifted the wrap, set it back down immediately, and told the nurse to call the hospital and get the operating room ready. *Now!*

I went into surgery right away. Before they put me to sleep the doctor said, "Dick, what you have is a terrible infection. Remember that's always been my worst fear. If it's into the bone, we're going to have to take your leg. Otherwise the infection can spread through your whole body and kill you."

I didn't care. I was tempted to say, "Cut if off right now." I was that sick. It hurt that much. I'd never been this sick in my life. Everything hurt. Opening my eyes hurt.

After surgery I heard the nurse say, "Richard, Richard, open your eyes." "I don't want to," I groaned. "Is my leg still there?"

I opened my eyes.

It was still there.

Eight to ten hours more, the doctor said, and the infection

would have been into the bone. There would have been nothing they could have done.

I thanked God I got sick on a day I was supposed to have physical therapy. I thanked God Julie didn't just say, fine, you have the flu, see you next time.

It saved my life.

I had IVs in both arms and was in isolation to keep from getting another infection.

December 12, 1989.

I was lying in isolation, thinking about the tradition I started so many Christmases ago when I was a kid: going out and cutting down a tree. Now my family was at home, with no tree and no presents. We had no money. Mr. Positive was having trouble feeling positive. Just when I was about to die of despair, I got a phone call.

A whole crew of people from the American Lung Association Running Club in the Twin Cities had cut down a Christmas tree and taken it to our house. They took it inside, decorated it, and piled presents everywhere—presents collected from so many people, for Mary and Andy. And the food! All the food, it was really something.

I didn't know that right away, of course. All I heard was my son on the phone, hollering, "Pop! You should see all the presents! They're all the way up to the ceiling! I got a teddy bear—" and he went on and on.

Andy turned the phone over and now everyone was singing Christmas carols to me.

I was bawling. I couldn't speak. I was just sobbing into the telephone.

I was in isolation for more than two weeks before I could go home again.

Dr. Schmidt had given me a chart that projected how well I should be functioning after so much time. He said it was going to take twelve to eighteen months before I could do much.

It took closer to *two weeks*. Within two weeks I was back out in the barn, hobbling around. I knew I shouldn't have been, but I couldn't *stand* to be inside not helping with things. I was milking cows with a brace on. I couldn't bend my leg and wasn't very graceful. I constantly slipped in cow manure. The cows would kick me, and I'd slip and fall again. I was quite the sight.

I'll never forget taking my brace off for the first time. Those first few steps were scary! Without the brace I felt weak, vulnerable. I looked in the mirror. My left leg was like a bird leg, a pole with loose skin wrapped around it. I laughed, *hard*. It looked so funny! It was just a bone, that was it. I thought, boy, and I've been doing leg lifts. I had a long way to go.

As I started to walk more and more without the brace, my leg hurt because there wasn't much muscle there. It ached. I knew it would get better, but it was taking time . . . and lots of hard, hard work.

Within six weeks I was driving myself to the hospital for physical therapy. One day a high school teacher was there the same time as me. He was getting rehab after some minor surgery. I was frickin' running up and down the halls, practically, compared to him. He said, "Look at you! You about had your leg torn off and here *I* can hardly walk. It doesn't make sense!"

It did to me.

I clawed my way back doing leg lifts. They were my passion. I was *possessed* by them.

It reminded me of training for marathons. If a coach told me to run twenty miles I'd think, okay, twenty-five will be better. That can get you into trouble, I know. Trying to do too much too fast was probably what caused the farm accident. But I was doing everything I could to recover as quickly as I could.

That meant an *insane* amount of exercise. I was possessed by *hard work*.

I had great doctors and an excellent physical therapist. But the most important reason I got so much better so much faster than anyone predicted was this: my desire to get better and my willingness to work at it. I was going to do whatever it took to get back to normal and I was going to do it *now*.

There was no secret to my recovery. It was just hard, hard work.

Most people don't survive the kind of farm accident I survived. You can't believe the *power* in a power takeoff. I was lucky in that I was being beaten into the ground—even though it was frozen—rather than into concrete. A lot of guys, when they unload silage, they'll pull up onto a big concrete slab by the silo. With a power takeoff slamming you into concrete, you're about done for the first time your head hits it.

I don't think luck was the reason *I* survived, though. I think God truly had a purpose. I think he wanted me to speak about this accident and help make farming a safer profession. I was already a motivational speaker. People recognized me from my running and I had the potential to reach a wide audience. So many folks are injured or killed in farm accidents, and now I had the chance to help change that.

Maybe it would ease some of my discomfort at how much money was raised on my behalf. Tens of thousands of dollars were donated after a fund was established at a local bank. How do people who aren't well known get by? I wondered. It really bothered me. I couldn't do anything about that, but I could spread the word about farm safety. A professor or university extension agent rattling off farm safety statistics gets boring. I knew it would be a different story when I told mine. And I didn't plan on ever turning down an invitation to speak about this.

I knew I'd already saved lives, because people would write to me and tell me that. A guy from Chicago, for example, said he was going to commit suicide—until he heard about my accident. Just like that, he changed his mind! He wasn't even a farmer.

Another guy, who lived about five miles from where we did, always ground feed wearing this old, torn jacket. His wife had been on him for a year to get rid of it. They heard about my accident on WCCO Radio out of the Cities, and he went to his closet immediately and threw the jacket away. Maybe I saved his life. His wife wonders.

It was hard to know how much my story was inspiring other people. I knew one thing: I owed something back.

May 17, 1990. Grantsburg, Wisconsin.

Grantsburg is near where we lived and I almost felt like I was from that town, we had so many friends there. Their cards and letters and prayers—like the best wishes coming in from all over the country, all over the world—were an indispensable part of my recovery.

Here I was, less than six months after the accident, running again. In a race! It was only five miles, and I finished in about thirty-three minutes. But a Twin Cities TV station was there, and everybody was cheering.

I was third to cross the finish line, and as I broke the tape they had up especially for me, the emotions welled up again.

I was back.

In a *Runner's World* feature, "The Best of 1990," I was named Comeback Runner of the Year. I'd also been named to the Road Runners Club of America Hall of Fame.

I recovered so completely from the accident that by September 1991 I was ready to run a marathon, the North Country Marathon in Walker, Minnesota. It was mostly through the woods. I ran it more on memory than anything, because I hadn't been doing any hard training. At about eighteen miles we got on a long bike path and I could see all these guys in front of me.

Gee, I thought. They're not that far ahead.

I started taking them one by one.

At twenty-three miles a man at an aid station said, "Beards! You're in second place!" I could hardly believe it. I never saw the guy in first place. I couldn't get close to him. It was just as well. I was starting to hurt and just wanted to hold onto second.

Which I did. I finished in 2:53:42 and was *elated*. I'd proven something: the farm accident was *not* going to slow me down.

Fine, the heavens seemed to say. We'll find some other way to do it.

Sunday, July 5, 1992. I was driving home with Mary and Andy after appearing at a race in La Crosse, Wisconsin. We were on a county road near River Falls when out of nowhere a woman in what looked like a Jeep pulled out from a side road. She was going to hit us! I tried to go around her but her vehicle clipped ours on the side and spun it around. We went into a ravine and landed in a pasture. I got out to check on Mary and Andy. They weren't seriously hurt, but I felt dizzy. They took me to the hospital. I had back and neck injuries.

My first taste of heavy-duty narcotic pain medication was after the farm accident, but I got more of it now. Here I was, back in the hospital, all busted up again. A lady runs a stop sign and life is chaos once more. I had trouble coming up with a positive spin on it. Then I thought about the drugs. They were something to look forward to.

When I was discharged, I got a couple of prescriptions for Percocet, which I filled and took as directed. I went back to the doctor for a checkup and they told me this would be my last prescription. After that I was supposed to take Advil or whatever. Fine.

The day I was supposed to get my last prescription filled, I was anxious. The last pills! I found a copy machine and ran the prescription through it, my heart racing. It looked like a copy, though, not even close to the real thing.

I couldn't let anyone see this. I sat in my truck, took the cigarette lighter that had never been used, and burned the copy.

I filled the prescription. My back was killing me. My neck was, too. They were really stiff, but I was determined to tough it out after the high-powered meds ran out. I gave Advil a chance. Eventually the pain subsided somewhat, and I came around.

I tried not to think about how much I'd wanted that copy to come out cleaner. I was just concerned about Mary, I told myself. I had to get back to doing as much on the farm as I was before, so it wasn't all on her again.

It was no use. I couldn't farm in this kind of shape. We'd been independent contractors on this place, and I was still hoping to buy it one day. Now we told the owner, that's not going to happen.

We got out of farming, this time for good.

For a while now I'd been told that since I'm such a yakker, I should consider farm broadcasting. It sounded fun. I moved the family to Crookston, where I became the farm director at a local radio station. It didn't pay much, but we were used to that. Mary got a job at a bank right away, which helped.

Mary was all for moving this time. She was so glad to be off the farm! Even today it makes me chuckle, how little she tried to hide her disgust at our situation—even in interviews. You watch a tape and think, this woman is not happy.

Six months after the car accident I was covering a farm show in Fargo. After work I went out for a run as usual. It was snowing and the roads were really icy, but that didn't stop me. I was running along, and—*oh my God!!*—it was like someone just swung at me, full power, with a baseball bat. I'd been hit by a truck or a van and the driver didn't stop. Maybe they didn't see me, it was snowing that hard. But I was *hurting*.

I was in the hospital with back and neck injuries again, and once again I was on pain medication. I wasn't going to turn it down, but it wasn't like I was having fantasies about it either. When they started me on Demerol I thought, that's fine. I was very agreeable to it, that's all.

They discharged me and put me back on Percocet. I was in such rough shape I stayed in bed most of the time. I'd been home less than two weeks. Mary was home for lunch like always—the bank where she worked was nearby—and I headed upstairs to lie down after talking to her. I got to the top of the stairs and . . . maybe it was being in bed all the time, maybe it was the meds, but . . . I was so dizzy . . . and . . . I fell down the stairs! These old wooden stairs. I was lying there at the bottom of them, a crumpled mess.

Mary called an ambulance, which took me to the hospital again. A neurosurgeon saw me right away because I'd landed on my neck. This was not good.

I was in *so much pain.*

They told me I could get a pain shot every few hours and I took them up on it. Every few hours I pushed my call button and they obliged.

I'd been in the hospital a few days when the neurosurgeon paid me another visit, but this time he didn't look like he cared how I was feeling. My bed was next to the window and the doctor pulled the curtain closed, the one between me and my roommate.

"You know what, Beardsley?" he said, not a hint of compassion in his voice. "I think you're addicted to painkillers."

I looked at him, wondering if he thought this curtain was keeping the other guy from hearing every word.

"You wrecked up your back," he continued, "but you've been asking for these pain shots like they're going out of style."

I was ticked. Don't tell me I can have something that will take the edge off the pain, I thought, and then accuse me of being a drug addict when I accept.

"Cut me off then," I snapped.

He told me how they planned to wean me off the drugs, a plan that included methadone. "Methadone is a narcotic," he said, "but it also helps people who are using a lot of drugs to get off of them. Just take it like I prescribe. . . ."

He left. I thought about what he said.

I am *not* lying here wanting a buzz, I thought, crying.

I kept thinking.

The doctor had a point, not that I was interested in telling him that. The physical pain wasn't so unbearable I couldn't make do with less medication. But Mary and Andy were home without me again, the bills were piling up with no prospects of getting paid, and pretty soon—I'm human—I just craved a little relief from the stress. The stress of wondering when all this would end.

Always before when stress piled up I'd just go for another long run. Now I didn't have that—crutch. Wow. I'd never thought of running that way. Maybe I had been compulsive about it. How else do I explain my absolute refusal to take a break unless an injury forced it?

Nobody ever criticized me for being compulsive about running when I was winning marathons. Nobody ever sat me down and said, "I think you're addicted to running," like I was some sort of loser.

I missed the feeling of well-being I got from the hard training. I missed it desperately.

And I had to admit, artificial as it was, the high I got from the painkillers was the closest I came to it.

I got out of the hospital and slowly got back on my feet again. I was still wondering when my string of misfortunes would end . . . when it didn't.

Two and a half weeks after falling down the stairs, I was returning home from a speaking engagement in the Cities. It was snowing, it was blowing, typical for Minnesota. Andy was asleep in the back of the Bronco. All of a sudden there was a whiteout, and the wind! Before I knew what was happening, the wind caught us and *slammed* us into a snowbank. Now the truck was rolling!

Everything happened so fast. Andy was thrown from the Bronco, still in his sleeping bag, miraculously in the opposite direction from where the truck landed.

I was stuck inside. Literally stuck. I could hear the ambulance. I was pinned between the door and the dash and the steering wheel.

They called for the jaws of life.

The jaws of life wouldn't work. It was too cold.

I spent another week or so in the hospital, this time with fractured vertebrae and head injuries. I wore a neck and back brace for six weeks.

By April I could run again, maybe half an hour, forty-five minutes a day— nothing too strenuous. I kept feeling better and better, and increased my mileage accordingly. In July I headed out for a run and had gotten about twenty yards down the road when it felt like someone had just *stabbed* me in the lower back. I couldn't stand up! I was all hunched over, and stumbled back to the house. I got in the truck and drove to the doctor right away. I couldn't walk very well, but I could drive.

The doctor referred me to a physical therapist and gave me a prescription for Percocet.

After two weeks my back hadn't improved at all, so I started seeing a specialist in Grand Forks.

In January 1994 I had major surgery on my back. It took twelve and a half hours. I was facedown the entire time. The anesthesiologist who was supposed to move my face from side to side every half hour never did. My eyes swelled shut, there was yellow pus running out of my skin, and some nerves in my face were killed. An attorney later told me I should have been compensated for the injury, but I waited too long to pursue it.

I was in the hospital for twelve days recovering.

My back got better, but I had a reaction to the hardware in it. In March I had more surgery to remove the hardware.

By May of 1994 I was addicted to painkillers, though I couldn't admit it. Looking back, that's the only way to explain what happened next.

I went in for a checkup and was excited. "I feel great!" I told the doctor. "I've been off pain pills for a month now."

"That's good," he said. "I'm glad you're feeling better." He paused. "You know, the kind of surgery you had takes twelve to eighteen months to really recover from. If your back starts to bother you, just let me know and we'll get you fixed up."

I was *not* turning this down.

"You know," I said. "My back does hurt once in a while. Maybe I should get a prescription from you now. . . ."

He gave me one for sixty Percocet. I walked down the hall to the pharmacy right there in the clinic and got it filled. I went out to my truck and took three right away.

Just like that.

I couldn't run after the back surgeries. Walking wasn't easy either. But I could bike.

I got into biking in a big way that summer. One day I was out for a ride, coming back into Crookston. I could see cars parked alongside the road up ahead. I looked over my shoulder to see if there were any vehicles coming so I could pull out onto the highway a little and go around the parked cars.

I was used to covering that distance on foot, not on bike. I didn't realize how much ground I was covering so fast because all of a sudden—pow!—I slammed right into the back of a brand-new Cadillac. I went flying over the Caddy and onto the highway. There was a car coming toward me and, for once, the worst *didn't* happen. The driver missed me.

I was rushed to the hospital. The doctor sent me home wearing the same plastic brace I had used after the back surgery.

I've always been accident-prone.

I had the usual broken bones as a kid, but as an adult, you'd swear I was doing this stuff on purpose. *I* swore I wasn't.

After the 1988 Olympic Trials, when we were living in South Dakota and I was working for Land O'Lakes, I broke my sunglasses. I was in my office that evening, trying to fix them with Super Glue. A box elder bug flew in my face and without thinking, I batted it away with the same hand I was using to apply the glue. The end of the tube caught my eye and—*oh no!! It glued my eye shut!!* It was working like crap on the glasses, but it glued my eye shut *immediately.*

I had two operations and was in the hospital about a week. The pain was excruciating, but then so was the embarrassment. They were training nurses and one afternoon I could hear the head nurse out in the hallway. Gals, she said, there's a guy in here who Super Glued his eye shut. You couldn't *believe* the laughter. At least it was a fleeting distraction from the pain.

To this day it hurts to think about it, the agony was that intense. I was constantly getting pain shots. My butt was so filled with needle marks, one time they had to go for my hip. The head nurse wanted to know if one of her rookies could give me the shot. Sure, why not? Except she hit my hip bone, bent the needle, and had to pull it out at a ninety-degree angle. I'd only *thought* I was in agony before. It was almost like she decided, you need a pain shot? I'll give you a reason to need one!

It reminds me of being at Bemidji State Park with Andy and one of his buddies a few years later. The sun was shining and it was a great day. I was on top of a cliff taking a nap while they were down below looking at rocks. "Hey Pop!" Andy called. "Come 'ere! I want to show you something." "Aw Andy," I moaned. "I'll never make it down there with my knee." I was having serious problems with it, and the last thing I needed was to start rock climbing.

"*Please,* Pop," Andy begged. He didn't let up. I gave in.

I was going for it, but the knee wasn't. It buckled and suddenly I was doing somersaults down the cliff. I almost hit a tree before I crashed over a boulder and toppled onto some rocks. I felt like a cartoon character, just not as lucky.

Andy's friend ran to the park ranger's office for help.

The guys from the volunteer fire department showed up and I thought, this is not looking good. They seemed really nice, but they didn't look like they were in very good shape. It was going to be difficult to get me—on a gurney now—a hundred yards back up this steep cliff.

They made a valiant effort. They huffed and puffed and slowly progressed up the cliff. They were so into the task they didn't notice that the strap across my chest had slipped. It was down around my Adam's apple and choking me! I couldn't breathe! I was turning blue . . .

I was foaming at the mouth when one of the firefighters finally looked back to check on me.

"*Guys!*" he screamed. "*Stop!!*"

They had a little rescue mission within a rescue mission and set off again.

We got to the top of the cliff, then had about a quarter-mile trek through some heavy brush. At least it was level. This should be a breeze, I thought, after what I've just been through. Apparently they thought so, too, because it was quite a while before they checked on me and—*this hurt!!* The brush was so thick I had a stick caught in my eye, they couldn't hear me hollering, and it took forever for them to notice.

I felt like I was being rescued by the Three Stooges.

It was almost like they decided, you need an ambulance? We'll give you a reason to need one!

Then there was the time one of my cows almost killed me, back on the farm in Rush City. It was two-thirty, three o'clock in the morning, and I was out in the barn helping a heifer get ready to calve. She was having trouble, so I called the vet. I was using pull chains for a better grip on the calf, to help get it out. I slipped and accidentally hit the cow next to her. *She* was not pleased and she kicked me just below my left temple. I was bleeding. I was lying there when the vet arrived, and he didn't know which one of us he should attend to first. He cleaned me up, looked me over, and told me to get to my doctor right away. About four o'clock that afternoon I finally made it in to see him and got a few stitches. A quarter of an inch higher, he said, and that would've been it. You sustain a hard enough blow to the temple, you're done for.

Every July for several years, I went back to South Dakota State to help Coach Underwood with his running camp. Maybe I should have passed in 1994, but it was hard for me to turn anyone down—especially one of my coaches.

I got out to SDSU and was teaching a class when I started having back spasms. I was standing up at first, then I was kind of leaning on a table, then . . . well, I couldn't even stand up. A couple of students helped Coach get me to the hospital.

A week went by and I was still in the hospital and eager to get home. The doctors didn't want to release me. I begged

Coach to help spring me and finally he gave in. He assured the hospital staff he'd get me where I needed to go. I couldn't walk, but I could drive. Coach just kind of propped me up in my truck and pointed me in the right direction.

I had an appointment with my doctor back home in Crookston, who said I needed more back surgery. My body had reabsorbed the bone mass they'd used for the fusion and there was nothing left. They'd have to open me up from the front *and* back this time, and fuse both sides of the spine. It was a more complicated procedure, and Doc referred me to the Minnesota Spine Center. "I can give you one more prescription for pain pills," he said, "but that's it, because you're going to be under someone else's care." I got two hundred Percocet before I left. They'll last forever, I thought.

I visited the Minnesota Spine Center in August. I did need surgery, they said, but they couldn't get me in until October. I was already out of Percocet. My back hurt like heck, and at one point I was having such spasms that Mary took me into the clinic. They gave me a shot right there.

Doctors were starting to refuse pain pills, and I was having to be more creative to get any. I called Grand Forks and talked to one doctor's wife. "He won't give you any more, Dick," she warned. "Listen," I said, "Mary's birthday's coming up. Her folks are going to be here and we're all going to Winnipeg. The way my back feels, I'm just going to drag everybody down."

She didn't say anything.

"Listen," I continued, "I won't ask again. I promise. I'll go back to a doctor here, but at the moment I don't have one," blah, blah, blah.

Maybe just to shut me up, her husband gave me forty more pills.

They were gone before the weekend was.

It was about this time I got a letter in the mail saying my services were no longer needed at the radio station. There was a reference to my back troubles in the letter, which from what I understand, could have led to legal troubles for the station had I pursued it. I soon had enough trouble at home to keep me from plotting much in the way of revenge.

For some reason I was stupid enough to postpone telling Mary about losing my job. "I'll just wait until after my surgery," I thought. "She has enough to worry about." I did tell my former coach, Bill Wenmark, who of course shared the news with his wife, who of course didn't know it wasn't okay to share it with Mary the next time they talked.

Mary wasn't one to come down on me for much, but she made an exception this time.

I was in the hospital after the scheduled back surgery in October when she confronted me. Good thing I'm here, I thought, because I'll need time to recover—from the butt chewing, not the operation.

The back surgery had gone fine, or so we all thought, until one day when I was home recovering and was in so much pain on my front side I couldn't stand it. Mary took me to the ER in Crookston. The on-call doctor put me on a pain pump and told the nurses to keep it as high as the sucker would go. The pain was that severe.

My regular doctor paid me a visit then. He came in and closed the door. Mary was with me. She listened to him tell me he thought I was addicted to pain pills. I was crying. I didn't believe it. "Listen," he said, "it's nothing to be ashamed of." He reassured me that over the next couple of days while I was still in the hospital I could get a few more shots, but they were going to try to wean me off this stuff. Meanwhile, he added, they wanted me to get an evaluation at a mental health clinic.

Nothing really came of that until a few weeks later. In November 1994, I was out of pills. I was lying in the tub trying to get comfortable, which was impossible given the

excruciating pain. I didn't know how to cope with it by myself.

I spent nine days at Glenmore Recovery in Crookston.
They wanted to keep me for thirty days so I could go through
the full treatment program. No way, I told them. I could beat
this one with willpower. Willpower has nothing to do with it,
they insisted. You don't know me, I fired back.

I got home and was fine for a few months. In the spring
of 1995 I bought a new battery for my boat and strained
some muscles trying to lift it out of the truck. I was in the
hospital for a couple of days after that and eventually got
more pain pills.

They weren't enough, though. They were never enough.

I grew progressively more desperate.

For a while now, I'd been scouring the papers looking for a
bait shop for sale. I'd decided to give my fantasy life a try
and make my living as a fishing guide. In May 1995 I saw an
ad for a bait shop in the Detroit Lakes, Minnesota, area—an
angler's paradise if there ever was one. I talked to Wenmark
about it. He had a guy come up and look at it and his company financed the deal. We were in business.

Mary liked Detroit Lakes and was excited to move. By
now she'd forgiven me for not telling her I'd lost my radio job.
She wasn't one to hold much against me for long. She found
a job at another bank and we eventually found a house in
the country to rent. My guiding business really took off once
I opened the bait shop. Things were looking up. Mr. Mis-
fortune, as I'd been dubbed, was turning his life around, I
told myself.

My right knee had been giving me fits for the better part
of twenty years now, ever since I'd slipped on some ice back
in junior college. I'd had several surgeries, but nothing had
helped for very long. This time, in October 1995, the surgery
was much more radical. I walked around with titanium rods
coming right out of the bone, two stainless steel halos keep-

ing them in place. The pain never let up. It hurt people just to look at it.

As much agony as I'd ever endured, this was worse.

Though it was nothing compared to what I felt after a phone call in early November.

It was Dad, and he had cancer.

CHAPTER 7

The Toughest Race

I KNEW IF I KEPT FORGING prescriptions, eventually I'd get caught. But getting caught was the last thing on my mind the morning of Tuesday, October 1, 1996.

The day started like most others, lying to Mary about something. This time it was why I couldn't be with her on the way into Fargo for some business we had there. I couldn't tell her I had to stop at the Wal-Mart pharmacy for more pills.

I walked in and handed three prescriptions to the counter gal who told me it would be ten minutes or so. I said okay. George, the pharmacist, had become my fishing buddy. Normally when he heard my voice he'd look up and say, "Hey, Dick, how's it going?" This time I waited for him to say hi, and the minute he looked up, I knew. He had this incredibly sad look on his face, and before he said a word, I knew I was in trouble. I felt the blood drain from my face. It felt like it was draining from my whole body.

George walked out from behind the counter, and very politely, very gently, took me by the arm and walked me down an aisle where there weren't any other customers. He looked at me and said, "Dick, Dr. Turner knows. He knows what's going on."

The first words out of my mouth were, "George, I need help."

I meant it.

Getting caught hadn't been on my mind lately, but getting help had been. Just in the last week the drugs had been making me sick. I wanted to quit, but I didn't know how. My body was starting to rebel. The meds weren't doin' it anymore. I didn't feel high from them, just sick. I was up to ninety pills a day. I couldn't keep that up. I wanted help. I came close to asking my friend Brad for help at different times. I stopped short, though. I wanted help, but I was afraid of it.

George took me back to his office and we made an appointment with Dr. Turner for four o'clock. He wished me well. I walked out to my truck where I had a few more pills, but I didn't take any. That surprised me. You'd think if something like this happened you'd just load up on whatever you had left, but I didn't.

I met up with Mary and said I had to talk to her about something. We sat in the car and talked. I told her everything. It was hard, but I knew I was in a lot of trouble. I also knew if I wanted out of trouble, I had to start being 100 percent truthful about everything, and I was. It was hard to tell her all this, but she'd been suspecting something for a while. It hurt her that I'd been lying, but she made it clear she wasn't going to bolt. That was a big load off.

I was in a lot of trouble, but I was also relieved. I felt so much lighter, the weight of hiding everything finally gone.

On the way to Dr. Turner's office with Mary, I thought about the first day I went to see him. He'd put me on some Percocet, which I'd been on before. I can still remember him saying we have to be careful. A couple of weeks on the stuff, no problem, but if a couple weeks turn into a couple months, I could get hooked on it. Obviously we don't want that to happen, he said. Oh that's for sure, I agreed, knowing I was already way past that point.

The first thing Dr. Turner said was, "Dick, I'm here to

help." He said he didn't want to press charges. "You're not a bad person," he told me. "You're sick and you need help." He told me the authorities had contacted him the day before and planned to arrest me. He'd told them not to. "I don't think he'll run," he'd said, suggesting they put up all the flags, notify all the pharmacies. He'd said he was sure I'd be coming in again in another day or two to get more pills.

He wasn't mad at me, just disappointed. "But Dick, I have to tell you," he said, "in the next room are people from Drug Enforcement. They had to be contacted because I could be in a lot of trouble. They just want to talk to you."

I'd been crying, though nothing compared with the flood at hearing *that*.

The officers came in. A federal agent and an agent from the region's drug task force. They were very polite. One of them said, "Dick, for the month of August you wrote prescriptions for more than fifteen hundred pills. When we see something like that, our first inclination is, the guy's selling them."

I heard that and started blubbering. "I swear I did not give away or sell any of those pills," I told them, sobbing. I didn't say this, but I thought, I was selfish. I wanted them for *myself.*

"I swear to God," I said, "every one of those pills went into *my mouth,* no one else's. No one even saw me taking them."

They had questions. Where did I get the prescriptions filled? How did I do it? How often? When they finished, Dr. Turner made arrangements for me to go to Fargo's Meritcare Hospital. They didn't have a detox unit, but they'd put me on the psych ward. Mary needed to get home, so an officer drove me to my truck. I gave him the rest of my pills, and showed him where I'd been keeping them—up underneath my dash.

I showed him my notebook. I had this little notebook filled with codes. Everything was recorded: what pharmacies

I went to, the date, the drugs I got—and it was in code so if
Mary or anyone else found it, it would look like a form I
used to order fishing tackle for the bait shop. I showed him
all my little prescription blanks, and my utility knife and
ruler so I could cut them nice and sharp.

The agent took me over to the emergency room so I could
check in. He shook my hand, wished me well, and said they'd
be in touch.

By now it was seven o'clock in the evening and I'd never
had a headache like this one. It had been almost twelve hours
without any drugs, probably the first time in about a year. I
felt like crap, mostly from this righteous headache. I got registered and talked to a doctor about being on a lot of pain
meds. I couldn't use the word *addicted*.

Before they could do anything about my headache they
had to draw blood, take vitals, stuff like that. They did all
kinds of tests and asked all kinds of questions. In between I
was lying in a dark room because the light hurt my eyes. I
thought about the mess I was in, and how I was putting
Mary and Andy through still something else.

I got a cold washcloth for my headache but that was it.
Eventually they took me to my room on the psych ward, a
locked floor. Finally about eleven o'clock a nurse came in and
gave me some Percocet and Demerol. They couldn't take me
off the drugs right away because my body could go into shock,
they said, and I could die. After the meds I started feeling
pretty good. The headache disappeared and I calmed down
a little. Just having the headache go away was so relaxing.

I dozed that night, but they were in all the time checking
my blood pressure and whatever else. The next morning I
met with four or five doctors and counselors in a large room.
They asked me questions and took notes. They told me they'd
keep me on this Percocet/Demerol combination for less than
twenty-four hours, then start me on different drugs and help
me get weaned off of everything.

I was in the hospital nine days. I met with counselors and

pain management doctors. I went to group meetings with other people on the floor. They had a variety of troubles—alcoholism, drug addiction, mental illness. They ranged from teenage to elderly. It was quite a group. I felt like I was in *One Flew over the Cuckoo's Nest*. It got back to some of my friends in Detroit Lakes that I was in the hospital and a few came to visit. They assumed I was here for my back, of course, and were a little wide-eyed when they saw me in the psych ward. I explained about the drugs and everything was cool.

It didn't bother me to be here. I was glad. I knew it was the first step toward healing. At least I couldn't hurt myself.

That had been really starting to bother me, toward the end. What a miracle it was I didn't just stop breathing one night in my sleep—or kill somebody while I was driving, or out on the boat.

They had me on methadone when I was discharged from the hospital, partly because I still had the back pain that got me started on this crap to begin with. I didn't abuse the methadone. I took it exactly as it was prescribed.

Meanwhile the drug enforcement people had been in touch. "Dick," they said, "you've cooperated with us 100 percent and we appreciate that. We've looked into every thing. You told us you didn't sell anything, and we can't see that you did."

They told me Dr. Turner's office didn't want me prosecuted, but the county attorney's office did. "One or two prescriptions is one thing," they said, "but because there were so many . . ." They told me they'd try to work it so it wouldn't become public record. "Oh that'd be great, that'd be great," I said.

It was wonderful being home with Mary and Andy again. Andy didn't say much, but he knew what was going on. He's a smart kid. He seemed glad to have me home. So did Mary.

The next night it was time for my first outpatient treatment session at Drake and Burau in Fargo. There were about fifteen people in our group. First we went around the circle and introduced ourselves. Each person said who they were and why they were there. By the time it got to me, I was sweating. I was nervous, and I didn't believe what I was about to say: "Hi, I'm Dick, and I'm a drug addict."

That hurt. Oh that hurt. I didn't even believe it and it hurt to say it. I couldn't picture myself an addict. An addict meant needle marks, no family, no job, doesn't bathe, lives on street corners. A big loser.

It took everything I had to get the word out.

Sue, our counselor, introduced me again and suggested I tell the group what had happened to me.

So I did. I cried. I didn't know what to make of all this. The rest of the evening I didn't contribute much. It was all so new.

It was fascinating, though. Everyone was in a different stage of the recovery process. It was my first night, but some people were graduating from outpatient treatment. Their stories were interesting. There was crying, there was screaming, but it was okay somehow. "What you say in this room stays in this room," they kept reminding me.

I sat there like a little kid, just watching everything. But it felt good, because everyone in the room had the same problem. We were all trying to recover from an addiction.

Outpatient treatment was three nights a week, Monday, Tuesday, and Thursday from six to nine o'clock. From six to seven o'clock all the small groups met together—there might be forty or fifty people in a big room. During that time, one of the counselors might lecture on something. Maybe we saw a video or had a guest speaker. Then there was a short break. People drank lots of coffee and smoked a lot of cigarettes. You may have heard the expression, the drugs won't kill you but the tobacco will. It could be forty below and almost everyone was outside smoking. I was one of the few who wasn't.

From seven to nine o'clock we were in small groups. At the start of each meeting we went around the circle and introduced ourselves, even if everyone already knew each other.

Then we said the Serenity Prayer, all together like we were in school. Then we went around the circle again, and each person read one step of the twelve-step recovery program. Then Sue asked if there was anything any of us wanted to bring up. If so, we raised our hand. Then she asked us, one at a time, if we'd done our assignment—and we talked about each one. Sue would say, well, what do you think about what this person just said? And people gave their opinions.

This is where it got heated. People got mad at Sue and they got mad at each other. Someone might say, "I think you're lying. You're hiding something." And you wanted to say, "F—— you, buddy, how would you know?" When people accused me of lying or holding back, I cried or shook my head. Sometimes I got so emotional I couldn't speak. There were boxes of tissue all over the place. Good thing.

You have to get on people, though. You have to tell the truth if you're going to get better. I had trouble getting on others, but I did sometimes. Because I learned to recognize when they were lying.

So it went on like this, and at the end of the meeting Sue told each person what she wanted accomplished by next time. At the end we stood up, held hands, and said the Our Father. If someone was graduating they got their little medallion, and everyone put their hands on the person. It was neat.

There was a really systematic way they worked us through the stages of recovery. I started on pain meds because of physical pain, but I stayed on them because I thought they were helping in other ways. I learned that addictions are usually a lifetime in the making and to free myself I had to get to the bottom of what hurt. I didn't do that the first night, of course, but other people were further along. They were telling their story to a family member or whomever, and it was so emotional.

The early stages of recovery are almost like what you go through when someone you love dies. There's a series of steps to help it sink in that you're really addicted, just as there are steps to help it sink in that the person you love is really gone. It takes a while for you to believe that you *are* an addict.

I was in group therapy, but I was also in one-on-one counseling. An hour a week, whenever I could work it into my schedule. *Those* were intense. Early on in one of them, Sue told me she didn't think I was taking this seriously. That stung! "I think this is just an act for you," she said. "You act like you're so happy all the time."

She thought it was an act, but it's who I am, addict or no. Later she realized it. As she got to know me, she realized I'm almost obnoxiously cheerful. I'm the person who can get on your nerves, I'm that upbeat.

She didn't buy it at first, especially when I told her I was still taking methadone. "Dick," she said, "I realize this is prescribed, but I'm having a big problem with it. It's a narcotic. You're coming here, but you're still under the influence. It would be like letting an alcoholic come here three nights a week after they've had a couple of beers."

"You know you're *right*," I told her.

"It goes against everything we're trying to teach you," she said. "What if you bring your pills tomorrow night and we dump them out?"

"Sounds good," I said, though I couldn't help wondering: what about my back?

We called Mary right away, and asked her to count how many methadone pills were left. Eighty, she said. I brought them back the next night, we counted them, then went into the men's room and flushed them down the toilet.

It felt good to do that, really good. I thought, okay, now recovery *really* starts.

I had trouble falling asleep that night. By three o'clock the next morning I was flopping around in bed. My arms ached so badly I thought I was going crazy. I got in the bathtub to soak. I was hot, I was cold, I was out of my mind I was so sick—and getting worse by the minute. It had been thirty-six hours since I'd had any methadone and everything *itched*, from the inside out, and I couldn't do anything about it. I couldn't get any relief and it got worse by the minute. I was going *nuts*.

About a quarter to four I called the emergency room at Meritcare and told them I needed help. The woman in the ER said to hold on until morning and call my counselor.

I called Sue first thing, who called Dr. Turner. They put me back on methadone. Sue said they'd just cut me off too quickly and should have tapered me down. So every day I took a little bit less, and a little bit less.

Three or four weeks into outpatient treatment, it hit me. I was in group, I was talking, I was listening to others talk, and all of a sudden—I don't know what, exactly, brought it on—it hit me.

I am a drug addict.

Just like that. Always before, I could accept that I was in treatment, but that was it. I wasn't an addict. All these other people were. I was dependent on medication, but I wasn't an addict. To say I was, at the beginning of each meeting, was the worst. I forced myself. I only said it because I had to.

Suddenly I realized I'd spent those first few weeks in group being defensive. Between Sue and everyone else, they were just so brutally honest. People said this or that about me, and I wanted to tell them they were full of it.

It was early November, and it had taken me about a month, but I could finally say it and *mean* it: I am a drug addict. I told the group it had dawned on me, I *am* an addict. I believed it now. And you know what? From that moment on it never bothered me.

Hi, I'm Dick Beardsley, I'm a drug addict. It rolled off my tongue. I was neither proud nor ashamed. It's who I am. Admitting that was my first step toward getting better.

When I first told Mary about the addiction, I was truthful instinctively. Now I knew why truth was so important. Recovery is peeling away all the layers, getting to the bottom of everything. Your counselor, the people in your group, all of them help you realize the defenses you've been putting up and the way you've been hiding behind them. Unless you're brutally honest about what hurts, you won't be able to learn how to handle the hurt in a healthy way.

It's not for sissies, though.

I fancied myself an easy person to get to know, nothing to hide, that sort of thing. I found out I'm really open with people *to a point,* but there are plenty of things I didn't care to talk about. I wasn't interested in talking about the intimate part of my marriage, for example.

"Too bad," Sue said.

I was never in the service, but I felt like I was in boot camp. From what I hear, in boot camp they break you down so they can build you back up. I thought that was what was going on here. It almost seemed like they did things in treatment just to make you angry. It forced you to open up, and everything spilled out.

Sue wanted to know about the intimate part of my marriage, and I found out how reserved I can be. I did *not* want to talk about that. There wasn't anything *to* talk about, for one thing. For several months now, Mary and I hadn't been close, not that she hadn't wanted to be. I was afraid things wouldn't work because of the drugs.

I'd made up every excuse to avoid her. I'd lied to her about everything, this included. "My back hurts too much," I'd tell her. "I'm too tired." I told her everything except the truth. She hadn't known about the drugs, and wondered what was going on. She worried she wasn't attractive to me anymore. I didn't know if she worried about an affair—it had never been an issue with either one of us—but if there was ever a time she questioned my devotion to her, this was it. She knew I was pushing her away, but she didn't know why.

I didn't know how much I was hurting her. I was too consumed by the drugs. Getting them, hiding them, getting some more. "How's Mary?" someone might say. "Heck, Mary and I are doing great," I'd tell them.

Sue knew better.

She helped me see how I'd been neglecting Mary and Andy. How selfish I'd been. I thought I was fooling everybody, that everything was fine. Wrong, wrong, wrong.

An addiction can make you very selfish. When I was abusing drugs, my concern was me. My body was with my family, but nothing else. I wasn't able to support them. I wasn't there emotionally for Mary or Andy, not at all.

Through both group and individual therapy, I learned I have an addictive personality. Because both of my parents were alcoholics, I vowed I would never become one and I didn't. But they say that as the child of alcoholics, I had an 80 percent chance of becoming addicted to something.

People with addictive personalities, I learned, are compulsive about whatever it is they do. Mary and Sue both think I'm compulsive about running. Granted I get up at three-thirty every morning to run five miles no matter what the weather and no matter how tired I am. I don't think that's compulsive. Nobody ever accused me of that when I was training for the Olympics. They promote exercise in recovery, and that was the easiest step for me to follow. I like how running makes me feel, and it's as natural as brushing my teeth. Plus if I miss a day of running, it's no big deal. If I would have missed a day of pills, oh my God, I'd be screaming at people I'd be going that crazy.

Another thing that became clear during all this was my tendency to let people walk all over me. It used to be, someone would ask me to do something and I'd drop everything to help out, no matter what was going on. Now I still help, but maybe more at my convenience. Or at work, if someone blames me for something going wrong and it's not my fault, I'll stand up for myself. Compared with someone who's assertive, I'm still a pushover, but I'm a lot better than I was.

The thing is, I fancied myself as this person who could blow everything off and never let anything get to me. But it wasn't true. It was a problem if, at some level, I was stewing about it. Pretty soon I couldn't even remember why I felt bad, I just did . . . and a pill made it better. Little things piled on top of each other, no big deal in and of themselves, but they added up.

In treatment I learned that if someone's out of line, there are ways you can gently point that out. Put the yuck stuff where it belongs, back on the person who's creating it. You can be a nice guy and stick up for yourself at the same time. It doesn't have to be one or the other.

Don't get me wrong. I'm not Mr. Aggressive now, far from it. But if someone's driving me crazy I at least say, "Calm down, relax, things'll be fine." Before I wouldn't even say that much.

I get teased a lot, which is okay. But it feels good to have this line that people had better not cross. In recovery they call it having boundaries.

Weeks went by, and I was starting to get it. I was an addict. I'd been neglecting my family because of it. And I was going to have to learn to have more of a backbone.

A lot of people in recovery have to get a new set of friends because their existing friends are users. If they're not assertive, their old friends will be their undoing. You need people around you who will support the changes you're making. I was lucky. I didn't drink, and none of my friends were drug users.

I was lucky in a lot of ways.

I was alive, I was getting better, I was feeling like my old self again.

The only problem, from my standpoint and for all I knew from Sue's, was that I was still taking drugs. The first time they tried to taper me down off the methadone, the withdrawal was just as bad as when I tried to quit cold turkey.

So we tried again, tapering down more gradually. It still didn't work. And again. You get the idea. One of these days, I was told, I might have to resort to inpatient treatment for help in getting off the crap.

I wasn't looking forward to it.

CHAPTER 8

The Road to Recovery

GETTING CAUGHT FORGING PRESCRIPTIONS was one of the lowest points of my life, no doubt. But it was a Tupperware party compared to finding out the story was about to go public.

It started with a phone call from a reporter Friday morning, December 6, 1996. "Dick," he said, "I just found out something and wonder if you could verify it." Sure, I said. He wanted to know if I was the Richard Beardsley cited in a court complaint.

I couldn't answer. I was speechless. I just sat there. I didn't know what to say

Finally I asked him how he found out. "Well," he said, "are you the one?"

I paused. "Yeah," I told him.

The last *I'd* heard, this was not going to be public record. I was stunned.

The reporter pressured me to go on the air with him, right then, to tell people what was going on. My first instincts were, darned right I'll do that. I wanted people to know I was hooked on painkillers versus selling drugs to kids.

Then I thought, wait a minute, why is this guy so eager

to get me on the air? I didn't trust him. I told him I had to call some people first.

I called Sue. "I have no idea what to do," I said.

"Dick," she said, "do *not* say a word. Don't say *anything*. I know you want to, but don't." She suggested I get a lawyer.

I called the reporter back and told him I couldn't say anything.

"Oh, just a little something," he pleaded.

"No," I said, "I'm sorry. I can't."

He didn't let up. He kept trying to talk me into it. He was yakking away and all I could think of was how to get rid of him. Then it occurred to me to ask *him* something.

"You're not going to send this down the wire?" I asked. If he gave the story to the Associated Press, I was done for.

"I have to," he said. He said if he didn't, someone else would and he wanted credit.

"Well, you've gotta do what you've gotta do," I said, and hung up.

I called Bill Wenmark, who made some phone calls and called me back. "Don't say a word to anybody," he warned. "Do not talk to the media at all." He'd been in touch with Tom Kelly and said he was one of the best defense lawyers in the state. "He's agreed to take your case," Bill said, "and he's not going to charge you."

Tom called that afternoon and told me not to talk to the press. "Let me handle things," he said. "If anyone calls, here's my number. . . ."

I spent the rest of the afternoon at my friend Brad's house. He'd been through treatment, though not in the public eye. We talked. I thought, this is the worst nightmare of my *life*.

I went home. Mary was just getting home from work. "Rich . . ." she said. The only time she calls me Rich is when she's feeling really good toward me. "You know, Rich, hang in there . . ." she said, not knowing what else to add.

By now the phone was ringing constantly. Ring, ring, ring.

Mary took the calls and told everyone I couldn't talk. The phone rang all evening.

I flipped through the channels on the TV, all the Fargo stations. Every one ran the story.

I was supposed to leave early the next morning to drive to Rockford, Illinois. I was scheduled to speak at the Rockford Road Runners' annual Christmas banquet. I did *not* want to go.

I couldn't sleep that night. This was so much worse than getting caught forging prescriptions. Now my whole family was being humiliated.

I got up early the next morning and drove to the Holiday station in town to get newspapers, the Minneapolis *Star Tribune* and *The Forum* of Fargo-Moorhead. No one at Holiday said anything so I thought there was probably nothing in the papers. I went out to my truck, got down the road a little ways, and pulled over. On the second page of the state section of the *Star Tribune* was the headline, "Beardsley Charged with Forging Drug Prescriptions." There was my picture. If you just looked at the headline and didn't read the story you'd think I was selling cocaine or something.

Fargo paper, same thing.

The drive to Rockford was hell. I stopped in different towns along the way and bought copies of the local newspapers. Every one had a story about the drug charge. Every newspaper! Every radio station I tuned to was running the story.

I'd never been this depressed in my entire *life*. I got more depressed with every mile. I wasn't tempted to commit suicide, but decided there would be worse things than getting in a fatal traffic accident.

I called Mary from somewhere in Wisconsin. She said she didn't even recognize my voice. I was that down.

I was supposed to drive all the way to Rockford that night and have dinner with the race director. I called him from Madison and told him I was too tired, that I'd get a motel room and see him the next day.

The TV cameras were waiting for me the next morning at the YMCA where I was supposed to speak. "I can't say anything, I'm sorry," I told the reporters, wondering what the people in the audience were thinking.

Those three or four hours were some of the longest of my life. There was a 5K race followed by a big buffet luncheon. I chatted with people and no one said a word about the media. I gave my talk. They wanted to hear about the Boston Marathon. I entertained the crowd, and forgot about things a little while I was speaking. Actually I did pretty well, considering how distracted I was.

Afterward I thanked God it was over.

The ride home wasn't any easier than the ride down. I got to the Wisconsin Dells, checked into a motel, and called Mary again. I was sick from despair. I felt like crap.

The next morning I didn't want to go home. I wanted to fill my gas tank and drive somewhere to hide out for a while. I stopped in Osseo, Wisconsin, to call Mary again. This time I felt so lousy I didn't even know if I'd make it home.

I did, though, later that afternoon.

The next day was a one-to-one meeting with Sue.

She sat me down and said, "Dick, first off I want to tell you this. What you're going through right now is *tough*. The vast majority of people who enter treatment have it known only to their families and close friends. Most of the time, nobody else finds out. Unfortunately because of your running career, it's big news. The whole world knows now."

She continued. "It's not going to be easy. But I want to tell you this: *you* know you're a good person. You made a mistake. You're making amends. You're in treatment, you're making progress, your wife and son know who you are and they love you. They know what you stand for. It *doesn't matter* what anybody else thinks, so try not to worry about it too much."

It was soothing to hear this. I love Sue. She knew when to kick me in the butt, and she knew when to give me a hug. She gave me a hug that day. She said she cried when she saw the story on TV.

I tried to tell myself it didn't matter what people thought, but I couldn't leave the house for about a week. I couldn't make myself get gas in town or go to the grocery store. I felt like I had a big "A" for addict on my forehead.

Soon there was a certified letter in the mail saying I had to appear in court. Tom Kelly sent one of his partners, Phil Jacobson, up from the Cities. We walked into the courtroom and it took about two minutes. All they did was read the charge against me: one count of fifth-degree controlled substance crime. All the TV stations were there and the attorney said, "Dick can't comment on this right now." Andy was with me in court and he was pretty impressed by the TV cameras.

It hadn't been easy for him in school, though. Rumors flew that I was dealing cocaine. He refused to wear anything with my name on it, or the name of my bait store, Beardsley Sports Center. For the first couple of days after the news broke, he wouldn't even go to school he was so ashamed of me.

The phone never really let up. Paul Levy from the Minneapolis paper called and said he wanted to do a story. He's a friend. I told him I couldn't say anything. He said, "Well, listen, I'm not going to include anything that will get you in trouble." I trusted Paul. He said he only wanted to clarify things, and it didn't sound like he was just out for himself the way the first reporter seemed to be.

I granted him permission, and the story ran in the Sunday edition of the *Star Tribune*.

The story was fine, but oh my God I'd known Bill Wenmark for almost twenty years and I'd never seen him so mad.

He called me and just laid *into* me for talking to the press. He stayed mad, too. Tom Kelly apparently calmed him down, because he let up after a while. Tom said there was probably nothing in the article that was going to hurt me.

I think the first time I left the house was for another trip to the Holiday station. Tim, the manager, said, "Dick, boy, you know they're raking you in the papers, but listen, we don't think anything different of you. You're one of the nicest people who walks in here, and we support you 100 percent."

And boom, just like that, I was fine. I didn't have to worry about being in public. I would be forgiven for this.

My next stop was the grocery store. Everyone I saw there was just as nice as Tim had been. Everywhere I went, the same thing.

I had people coming up to me, pillars of the community, who would pull me aside and tell me they had been there. They'd say, you know Dick, I have twenty years of sobriety, I went through treatment for alcoholism, I was addicted to pain pills in college, whatever. People I would never have suspected had this kind of problem were going out of their way to tell me they did.

You could almost tell by looking at them, though, they were really glad they didn't have to endure what I was, with everything in the papers and all.

The mayor told me there was nothing but support for me as far as he was concerned. Same with everyone at the Detroit Lakes Regional Chamber of Commerce. Everyone in town was so incredibly nice.

I was so glad I'd owned up to taking the pills, forging the prescriptions, all of it. I was the first to admit I'd made a terrible mistake, and people seemed to respect that.

Of course, I also heard about some who were snickering behind my back. That's *their* problem, I decided.

This was a good test of my recovery. I'd made a big mistake and I deserved to get beaten up a little bit. I was harder on myself than anyone else was anyway, except maybe Sue.

It also occurred to me that once I got some sobriety behind me, maybe some good could come from this. Maybe I could talk to kids about something more important than sports: staying free of drugs. Maybe they would listen to me. If the all-American kid—who never got into trouble, never drank, never even smoked—could become addicted, maybe he was worth paying attention to.

I knew it was way too early in my own recovery to give speeches about it.

I continued to be amazed by the kindness extended to me. Coach Squires sent a check for a thousand dollars with a note: "You've overcome worse than this. Just pretend like it's Heartbreak Hill." Coach had been great about staying in touch. He always told me to say hi to Mary and Andy. "Give my best to Sam and Spike," he always added, which cracked me up. Those dogs had died so many years ago.

My second court appearance was the Friday after Christmas. I pleaded guilty to the charge, then got fingerprinted at the county jail. More TV cameras followed my every move. "Gee guys, don't you have anything more interesting to cover than this?" I asked. "I know, Dick," one of them shrugged, "but this is our assignment for today."

Getting fingerprinted is humiliating enough without having it on TV. And of course on the news that night they showed me walking *into* jail, but they didn't show me walking back *out*.

The jailer getting my prints looked familiar. "You're not the guy who does that commercial for Paradiso?" I asked. Paradiso is a Mexican restaurant in Fargo. "Sure am," he said. I couldn't believe it. He was the guy who says, "Chips are free. Dinner's extra." He helped me forget being on TV myself for a moment.

With my second court appearance behind me, the attorneys decided it was time for a news conference. Monday, December 30, at the Holiday Inn in a Minneapolis suburb. Just before that I did a live interview with John Williams of WCCO Radio.

The news conference was difficult for me. Here were all these people who had covered me when I was running, when things were great, or after my farm accident. Everyone was really nice. The questions were about what you'd expect, nothing mean. People who saw the Twin Cities reports said they were tasteful.

Afterward I went one-on-one with some of the reporters, and by the time I left the Cities I felt like I'd just run four marathons. It was so *draining*. But I was glad the world was finally getting a chance to hear what I had to say.

I was so tired on the way home I had to stop twice for a nap in my truck. I was so exhausted I couldn't keep my eyes open.

The next morning I was on our hometown radio station's talk show, did a quick telephone interview with another Twin Cities radio station, and turned my phone off. I'd had enough of the media for a while.

I'd been in recovery since early October, and there was just one problem. I was still on drugs. The attempts to wean me off methadone had failed.

I was making progress in other ways, though.

About six weeks into outpatient treatment, it was time for me to tell my story. That was my assignment. I took most of the afternoon, went to a little coffee shop in the mall, and started writing on a yellow legal pad. I wrote and wrote and wrote. When I finished, I felt cleansed. It was good to see it on paper for some reason.

The next group session, I told my story.

I talked about my farm accident and my first taste of prescription painkillers. I'd never been on Demerol before, I said, and it was amazing how good it made me feel. Then there was the car accident in 1992, when I was put on a Demerol IV. "It was like seeing an old friend again," I admitted. I told them about my first attempt at forging a prescription that summer, and how much I'd wanted the copy to turn out cleaner.

Being off the drugs after that didn't bother me, I said, but I thought about them from time to time. After I was hit by a truck or van while running in that snowstorm, I was upset, but also kind of glad, because I knew I'd probably get some drugs—and I did.

I told them that after a couple of other accidents, hospital stays, and periods of being on pain meds, my doctor thought I was addicted.

"I should've faced facts then," I said, "but I thought I could stop on my own. Then in July of 1993 I went out for a run on my lunch hour. All of a sudden I was hunched over and could hardly walk or straighten up because of the terrible pain in my lower back. I saw a doctor, and he gave me some Percocet. It scared me to be on it after being off of it for a while, and I could've asked for an over-the-counter pain reliever instead. But I gladly took the prescription and used the pills. They helped my back, and I enjoyed how they made me feel."

I told them about the back surgeries, and my stint at the Glenmore Recovery Center, where I'd left and told everyone I'd beat this with willpower.

I told them about my knee surgery: "It was an excruciating ordeal, and I was put on Demerol in the hospital. Did I tell my doctor about my drug problem? No way. If I had, he might not have given me any medicine. I couldn't jeopardize that."

I told them about Dad having cancer, and how by then I was forging prescriptions. The doctor would give me a prescription for forty pills, and I'd mark one refill on the slip, so I'd get eighty. I couldn't believe I was doing that, but I was.

In early December 1995, I said, I went to Michigan to be with Dad during his surgery. I stayed at his house and one night I looked for some Advil in the medicine cabinet. I came across a bottle of Vicodin Extra Strength. I couldn't believe it! When my bottle ran out, I started stealing from my dad, who was dying of cancer. I justified it by thinking, well, he's getting pain medicine in the hospital.

By May, I told them, Dad was really bad off. He had two or three months to live. I couldn't handle the news. By then I was hiding pills from Mary. Life was, "How will I get more pills when these run out?" I knew Dr. Turner was about to have me quit the Percocet and that scared me.

In early July, I told them, I got the call from my sister that Dad was going downhill quickly. I needed to get out there. I didn't have much Percocet left, at least not enough to last me the trip. I didn't know what to do. The thought of buying drugs off the street didn't cross my mind. Even if it had, I wouldn't have known whom to ask. Then I remembered that Dr. Turner had given me the name of a pain management doctor in St. Cloud. He'd written the name on a prescription blank. I taped a little piece of paper over the name, made copies of the form, and wrote out a prescription for Percocet in Dr. Turner's name.

The first time was the worst, I told them. I thought for sure I'd get caught, but unfortunately I didn't. That first day I went to four different pharmacies and got a prescription filled from each one for sixty Percocet. I knew what I was doing was wrong. I knew I could go to jail, lose my business, possibly lose my family. But all that mattered to me was getting the drugs.

I told them I'd pleaded with God to just let me get by with this until after Dad died. Then I'd quit and get help.

Dad died at 2:45 the afternoon of Tuesday, July 16. I was very sad. It broke my heart to watch him suffer those last few weeks. But my thoughts quickly turned to my bottle of Percocet. I was taking about twenty-four a day at that point, and knew I didn't have enough left to last me until I got home from Dad's funeral.

When no one was around, I searched Dad's house for painkillers. Within two hours of his death my sisters had flushed everything down the toilet, I found out later. I'm sure they knew if they hadn't, I would have taken them.

I started having withdrawal symptoms and took it out on Mary and Andy. I felt awful. I couldn't wait to get home to write more prescriptions.

I told my group that I continued to forge prescriptions long after Dad's death. Not only for Percocet, but also for Demerol and Valium. My whole life revolved around the drugs. I was taking eight or nine Percocet, along with eight or nine 50-mg Demerol tablets, along with 5 mg of Valium . . . four or five times a day.

I told them I'd come home from a nonproductive day at work and fall asleep in my food. Those were the days I'd made it *in* to work. I was taking money from the business to buy drugs.

I told them I kept saying after this bottle is gone, I'll get help. But it took getting caught forging prescriptions to make me serious about that.

It took me a long time, but now I knew I truly was a drug addict.

This time, no one accused me of withholding anything. Several people had tears in their eyes. Sue was crying. She asked, "What do you think of what Dick had to say?" Nobody said much. "He said what he needed to say," was the most anyone offered.

What struck me as I read my story to the group was how many people I'd lied to. Probably the person I'd lied to the most was myself.

The next night, Mary came with me to group and I read my story again. We faced each other, and everyone was in a circle around us. Mary had been dreading this, I think. For one thing, she didn't know what I was going to say. For another, there were all these people she'd never met.

After I read my story to her, she got an assignment. A rebuttal. The next time we met, it would be Mary's turn to tell me *her* story. I found out later that not only did she not mind, she was glad. She was nervous, but thankful to have the chance to talk to me in an environment where I couldn't just walk away. Where I had to listen, where I couldn't get by with using the same old defenses and denials.

She said I was always trying to avoid listening to her. "You're good at it," she added.

The next meeting we faced each other with the group in a circle around us again. She was talking and I couldn't interrupt. *That* was hard. She talked and I tried to explain myself.

Sue jumped down my throat. "*You* be quiet!" she yelled. "This is *her* time to talk." I was used to getting yelled at in group, so that didn't bother me much.

I *wasn't* used to having to just sit there and listen to Mary rip on me. I wasn't allowed to say a word. I had to let her go at me, and boy, did she go at me. I had a reason for everything she brought up, and it hurt not being able to defend myself.

Mary was emotional at first, but after a while she got more into it. It seemed like she was glad for the opportunity to say, "You *hurt* me, Buddy, and now I'm going to make *you* hurt."

When we were living in Crookston, she said, and I went fishing in Bemidji, I had an accident and didn't call her. She sat and worried for more than four hours about me and Andy and Chris, Andy's friend. She finally got a call from someone she didn't even know, telling her about it. She was worried about me and felt angry and embarrassed for having to wait so long to hear what had happened.

I did the same thing last fall, she said, when I ran a race in Walker and hurt my back. The spasms put me in the hospital, and she had to hear about that from someone else.

She lit into me: "You don't return phone calls, you don't pay bills. You didn't even tell me when you lost your job a couple of years ago. I had to hear about it from Monica. I'm always the last to know everything."

She told me how often I'd have a fair amount of cash in my pocket, which was strange. When she'd ask why I had it, I'd tell her the bait store owed me money for something. "Now we know you were taking money from the bait shop to pay for prescriptions."

Many times over the past few years, she said, she'd ask me if I thought I was addicted to painkillers. I'd deny it and get very defensive. "This put me in an awkward position," she said. "How could I persist, and still have your trust? So I became less able to trust my own instincts or gut feelings about anything."

"When you'd sit in your chair every night and try to read the paper," she continued, "your eyes would be half-open and you couldn't stay awake or hold the paper up. Or you'd try to eat a bowl of cereal and spill it. I felt disgust and embarrassment. Why didn't you just go to bed? You weren't there for Andy and me anyway."

Then she talked about how I wouldn't be intimate with her, but wouldn't tell her why. "I felt lonely and empty and scared," she said. "I needed you. I had to deal with everything by myself and I didn't know how. What was I supposed to tell people who were forever calling about still some other bill that hadn't been paid?"

"I felt badly for Andy," she said, "when he'd ask you to

play with him and you'd either put him off or wouldn't give him your complete attention. He gave up on you. He'd ask me and I'd say, 'Ask your dad,' and he'd say, 'He won't.'"

Then she talked about a weekend we joined her parents in Fargo, when she caught me taking pills in the bathroom.

If Mary's goal was to hurt me, mission accomplished. I hurt terribly. She went on and on about how much everything hurt *her*. She said we were buried in money problems to begin with and I made them so much worse with the drug use. "It's always been your needs, your needs," she said. "You've been selfish. We've *always* done what you wanted to do. Always."

She was talking, and I was thinking, unless *you've* been addicted to something, don't tell *me* the right way to behave when you're in its grip. I kept wanting to butt in and say, you know, I didn't hurt you on *purpose*. I was helpless!

Mary didn't threaten divorce, but she said, "I've had it. If this happens again I don't know if I can be there for you. I wouldn't count on it." Later I thought about that and decided if this happens again, I don't deserve her. After I calmed down and really started listening, I thought, man, this gal really cares about me to have put up with all this crap.

She talked about fifteen minutes. I had plenty of time to think about what a jerk I'd been. Some of this I knew, of course. That's one thing about Mary. She's usually pretty good about telling it like it is. That night I could tell, though, there were things even she'd held back.

She disagreed: "This is the first time I've been able to get it all out! This is the first time you've been forced to listen to me."

Mary and I never argued about the things we talked about in counseling. In fact, I felt good on the way home that night. I felt really close to her. The yuck stuff had been around a long time, but we hadn't discussed it and it was keeping us apart.

Now everything was out in the open and we could deal with it. Together.

Reading my letter to Mary, and listening to hers: those were two major steps in my recovery.

Opening up and telling people about problems was never my style. I always kept them inside, even with Mary. If something bad happened, I wouldn't tell her because I didn't want her to worry. When more bills arrived, I hid them. That's the way I dealt with a lot of things, especially where Mary was concerned. I'd hide them and hope they went away. I didn't realize she worried more when she didn't know what was going on.

Now there was nothing to hide.

Not only that, but I was learning it's okay to share your problems sometimes. It helps. It makes you feel better just to talk and other people *can* help. I used to think it was a sign of weakness to ask. Now I realize it's a sign of strength.

Mary said the people in group were really hard on each other. Eventually she learned it was part of recovery, holding a person responsible for what they'd done. Outpatient treatment is intense. There's a lot of crying and a lot of shouting. I got angry a lot. I learned anger's okay, too. I got angry and then I got over it. I moved on. It's part of life.

I got angry in group because people told me things I didn't want to hear. It hurt to have my faults pointed out, to be criticized. It hurt, but I almost always went home and thought, you know, they're *right*. It's hard to change. People can be so stubborn. I'm as stubborn as the next guy.

Thursday, January 9, 1997. I took my last methadone. For twenty-four hours I was fine. But Friday night I didn't sleep very well. By Saturday I was going insane. Talk about irritable! This was the worst it had ever been. I was lying on the couch, just miserable. I wanted to cut my arms off, they ached so badly. My bones ached. I couldn't sit still. I was hot one minute, cold the next, hot, cold. I called Bill Wenmark and told him I had to get into inpatient treatment somewhere.

Bill had a friend at Fairview Riverside Recovery in Minneapolis and one of their counselors called me and said they could get me in the next day. Okay, I said, I'm ready. That night I didn't sleep at all. The next morning I was supposed to catch a bus about 6:30, but it was about forty below, my truck wouldn't start, and no one could come get me—so I missed the bus.

I was going *nuts*. I called the ER and told the doctor on call I'd been off methadone forty-eight hours, and was going down to the Cities that night for inpatient treatment. I didn't think I was going to make it, I added. He told me to come over to the hospital and they'd give me some methadone. I did, they gave me twenty milligrams, and within forty-five minutes I felt like a million bucks.

I arrived at Fairview that night.

The first thing they did was have me stand against the wall so they could take a couple of Polaroid mug shots. It was one o'clock in the morning, I was coming off methadone, and I hadn't shaved for days. I looked like . . . *a drug addict.*

The next morning I met with the doctor. He said, "Dick, here's the deal. I don't believe in the taper-down method for methadone." He said no matter how gentle the taper, at the end of it I'd still have withdrawal. "Methadone," he told me, "is one of the worst drugs to come off of, if not *the* worst. You're going to feel like you're going to die, you're going to feel like you *want* to die. But I promise you, you won't die." He said the next seven to ten days would be tough. They'd put me on some nonaddictive medication, but it was still going to be *tough.*

The understatement of all time, I soon realized.

How can I describe what it felt like to come off this stuff? Like I *itched, terribly,* all over, but I couldn't scratch. Or if I scratched, rather than relieving the itch, it got worse. I'd lie

in bed shaking, wondering how I was going to make it another *second*—let alone a few minutes, hours, or days. Everything ached. Everything hurt. After a while all I could do was
cry. Cry and be miserable. I'd take ten or fifteen baths in one
night, trying to get comfortable. It didn't work. Every nerve
ending in my body, it seemed, had been whacked off and
dipped in hot oil.

Even dressing myself in the morning was hell. Sometimes I
literally had to crawl on my hands and knees to get to a class
or a meeting, that's how much everything hurt. My days were
filled with lectures, group meetings, doctor visits. I was determined to show up for everything. I was going to beat this
frickin' disease.

I had excruciating headaches. I was so cold, I couldn't
wear enough clothes to keep warm. I was sick to my stomach,
I had diarrhea, I couldn't eat. I was confined to my floor because they were worried I'd go into shock. I wore a different-
colored wristband so they knew to keep a closer eye on me.

Finally, finally after about a week I started to feel the
slightest bit better. I could eat a little, sleep a little. Each day
it got a little better, to where one of the guys in our group
graduated from inpatient treatment and I was appointed our
group's leader. By now I could eat in the cafeteria with everyone else, and was able to go for walks and get a little exercise. I got to know the people in my group really well since
we were together all the time. At night there was free time,
but I took advantage of Narcotics Anonymous meetings. I
attended every one.

I read out of my Narcotics Anonymous book. I felt better
every day. Pretty soon Mary and Andy came for a visit. The
reason was we had to go through the same thing we did during the outpatient treatment. We had to tell each other our
stories in front of this new group.

"Nah, we've already done that," I told them.

"If Mary's able to come down, have her come down,"
they said.

They were right. It wasn't quite as emotional this time around, but it was a good review. It reinforced what we had learned several weeks ago.

One night while they were there, I got a pass and we went out to supper. It felt great to be with them and have a break from the hospital.

Two things occurred to me. One, how good it was for our marriage to go through counseling together. I think every couple might benefit from that, even if addiction isn't a problem. Two, I felt lucky I could have both inpatient and outpatient treatment. They were different experiences, but each reinforced the other.

I learned more about addiction, how it can happen and why, warning signs of a relapse, things like that. Mary learned what to look for, too.

One thing both groups conveyed to me was how it sometimes takes more than one time in recovery to *get it*. That scared me. Until now, willpower had gotten me everywhere. Suddenly it was ineffective. I guarantee you, if you think you can beat an addiction with willpower alone, you'll be back in trouble so fast.

Willpower has nothing to do with it. People don't say, well, if you would have just had more willpower, you wouldn't have gotten cancer. An addiction is a disease, just as surely as cancer is. It requires treatment, just like any other disease.

This was another revelation. That it was nothing to be ashamed of. I was emotionally and genetically predisposed to my addiction. To beat it, I had to learn how to deal with pain and anger and everything else. I couldn't mask the pain with pills anymore.

Drugs are a substitute for the real solution. That's why people use them, I imagine. It helps you forget about things you don't want to think about.

I had to look at myself honestly, look at the world honestly, and take responsibility for what I found out. *Being honest* and *taking responsibility:* those were critical to my recovery.

I graduated from inpatient treatment a few days earlier than most people do, after eighteen days, because I had outpatient treatment to return to. I went through the little ceremony, hopped on a bus, and came home.

But always, always, it seemed like there was just one problem. Two nights before I left Fairview I wet the bed. I was dumbfounded, but too embarrassed to say anything to anyone.

I got home, same thing. It started happening so often I had to wear those adult diapers. I talked to Mary about it and called a nurse.

During my inpatient treatment, I'd made an appointment for surgery in Minneapolis February 12. They were going to take the hardware out of my back since it had served its purpose and was probably the reason I was in so much pain all the time.

The hospital in Fargo called my back doctor and said there was something pressing on the nerve, adding that they thought the hardware should be taken out right away. Luckily the Twin Cities doctor had a cancellation and could take me the next day. We made the trip that night.

I made it clear to everyone in Minneapolis: I'm a drug addict, and I do not want to leave with any narcotics. Mary was my witness.

After surgery I was on a pain pump with Demerol for a couple of days. Dr. Denis came in and said, "I've never seen anything like it. When I cut into your back and got down where the hardware was, there was all this yellow liquid. It was infected. We were lucky. In twenty-five years of back operations, I've never seen anything like it. But we were able to get the hardware out, and everything looks good."

After surgery I reminded everyone that I didn't want to leave the hospital with narcotics.

The day I was to be discharged, I was waiting for Mary when this nurse came in. She gave me a prescription for

Percocet. A hundred and thirty of them! I didn't say anything, but I thought, I don't *believe* this. Another doctor came in and I asked, "What about this medication?" "Don't worry about it," he said. "Take it. It'll last you about three weeks. You'll be fine."

"Oh. Okay."

Mary picked me up. I was sore, so we stopped and got the prescription filled. Once we were home and I was able to stretch out, the pain wasn't really that bad. I took the Percocet anyway. Advil would have probably done it, but I opted for the Percocet.

The next day Mary took Andy to a Metallica concert in Fargo as a birthday present. I was alone. There were more than a hundred pills in the bottle. I was scared. I worried I might take them. I got out of my chair, walked over to the cabinet, got the bottle of pills, went into the bathroom, took the top off, and—I couldn't bring myself to flush them down the toilet.

I tried again, a little later.

Same thing.

I tried again, about five times in all.

Suddenly—I tried not to think about what I was doing— I walked over to the cupboard, grabbed the bottle, hurried into the bathroom, undid the top, dumped them into the toilet and flushed them before I had time to think.

I was proud of myself. I looked forward to telling Sue about this.

Sue was not impressed. "Can you believe that?" I asked. "I told everyone I didn't want to leave with narcotics, and *still* they gave me a prescription."

She looked at me.

"What?"

"Blaming it on the doctors, huh?" she finally said. "You told everybody you didn't want to leave the hospital with any drugs, and that's fine. But when you got a prescription for some anyway, all you had to do was rip it up and flush it down the toilet. It would've been over. Instead you took it, filled it, used some of it—and you're telling me you probably didn't even need it." She was glad I eventually got rid of it, but was really on me otherwise.

"You know what?" I told her. "I'm *glad* this happened. It proves to me I can't be in control of my own medication. I'm not an addict. I'm a super-addict." Outpatient treatment, inpatient treatment, for months I'd been working on this and the first time I was tested, I took more drugs.

It hit me: This was going to be a *daily struggle* for the *rest of my life.*

My first day of sobriety was February 12, 1997.

I continued the outpatient treatment, developing little rituals to help remind me I'd never lick the disease. There isn't a cure. I couldn't promise anyone I'd be sober tomorrow, only that I was right now.

I developed a routine I still follow years later. During my morning run I say the Serenity Prayer, followed by the Our Father. Then I say, "Lord, please help me through another day of sobriety. I'm so powerless over mood-altering chemicals, especially painkillers, that I need your help to go in the right direction, walk the right path, make the right choices. I pray and I hope you'll be here with me throughout the day. I pray for God, I pray for my family and friends and relatives. I'll talk to you tonight before I go to sleep."

I was sentenced on the drug charge March 28, 1997. The judge, who was very nice to me, asked me before the sentencing if I had anything to say. I told her I was extremely sorry for what I'd done and intended to make amends.

She said, "Apparently you've reached a compromise with the prosecutor." I could have gotten up to five years in prison and a ten-thousand-dollar fine. Instead I was sentenced to 240 hours of community service work, up to five years probation, and a thousand-dollar fine. I also had to pay eighty-seven dollars to Blue Cross Blue Shield because some of the medication went through on their health plan.

The judge said, "Mr. Beardsley, we've received an incredible number of letters on your behalf, with nothing but good things said about you. I know who you are. You've already been speaking to groups, you've already begun taking care of your problem. What would you say if, instead of that thousand-dollar fine, I add two hundred hours of community service, which you could work off by going out and speaking to more people?"

I gave her a big smile. "Judge," I said, "that would be absolutely wonderful."

She said, "Okay. That's the way it's going to be."

The prosecutor objected: "I think Mr. Beardsley should pay at least five hundred dollars of that fine."

"Well, thank you, Counselor," the judge answered, "but I've made my decision. Mr. Beardsley and I are happy with it, and that's the decision that stands."

I *was* happy. As happy as I could be, considering now I was a convicted felon. They told me if I got through my probation and everything went okay, the charge would drop from a felony to a misdemeanor. I wouldn't have the felony on my record.

Then I could go hunting again. Felons aren't allowed to carry firearms, at least not in Minnesota. I'd also be able to travel out of state without getting a travel pass. For now, though, if I wanted to travel outside of Minnesota or North Dakota, I had to get a travel pass from the probation office that said where I was going, how long I'd be there, and when I was going to be back.

I talked to my probation agent within a week of the sentencing. John had been doing this about thirty years. He told me, "I want you to be truthful with me. I've been at this a long time, and I have a good sense for people who are back using again. I'll ask you probably every time you come in here." Mary was with me that first meeting, and John told her to call him if she suspected anything.

He explained how probation works and said if after a couple of years I was still sober and had finished my community service work, they'd probably drop the rest of probation. It was up to me.

I graduated from outpatient treatment the end of April. The three-nights-a-week phase of treatment was over. I took advantage of what they call extended care, though, a one-night-a-week meeting for three or four hours. That continued until about the end of June.

I needed a sponsor, sort of a recovery cheerleader. They had to have been sober themselves for at least a year. My sponsor was my friend Brad. We didn't get together all that much, but we talked all the time. We were good buddies. If I slipped up, he'd be able to tell in a split second.

I also attended support group meetings whenever I could and stopped in and saw Sue in Fargo.

Since February, I hadn't really been tempted to go back on narcotics, though I was still tested from time to time. Now my mother was dying. At least when I visited her I didn't snoop in her medicine cabinet.

Early on in recovery, if I was driving and approached a town with a hospital, I'd look at the blue sign with the white "H" on it and have a flashback. I thought of being in the hospital and getting a shot of Demerol. If I knew there was a sign like that coming up I'd try to look the other way. I was afraid to be reminded of the feeling. It was a pleasant one. Euphoria. You got high, you felt really good, you were mellow. It was a fuzzy, light feeling of total well-being. I remembered it very clearly, and it was scary to look back on it.

Sue told me, "Dick, that's perfectly normal. It'll happen for the rest of your life, but it'll get less and less."

If my back hurt, I thought about the pain pills and how good they made me feel.

I didn't crave drugs. It's not like if someone would have come by and offered me a shot of Demerol or Percocet I'd be eager to take them up on it. Not really. I just got these little waves of déjà vu. The waves were gone almost as quickly as they came, and I was thankful for that. I'd say the Serenity Prayer right away and that really helped. Or I'd finger the medallions in my pocket, the ones that represented the various milestones of my recovery.

I'd been back in radio for a while now—once a yakker, always a yakker. One day at work a woman broke her foot on the ice in the parking lot and a couple of us took her to the ER. I stood next to her and the nurse brought her a shot of Demerol. She had this syringe with Demerol in it, and man, that brought back memories. Whenever I walked into a hospital I had that feeling, because everything smelled like drugs.

I hadn't met a test of sobriety that I didn't pass easily. But there were many days early on when I had to say the Serenity Prayer probably a hundred times. "God, grant me the serenity to accept the things I cannot change, the courage to change the things I can, and the wisdom to know the difference." There's no better blueprint for life, I have since decided.

Maybe being on drugs should be an ugly memory, but it's not. It's very pleasant. I'd be lying if I told you otherwise. Listen, this is powerful stuff. I'm a human being, and you think about the things that give you pleasure.

As the months went by, my speaking started to pick up again. The phone had stopped ringing once news broke about the drug charge. But by now publications like the *New York Times* had done stories, ESPN had run a piece, and a woman from Hollywood had called and wanted to talk to me about a movie.

More and more I allowed myself to think about how my mission in life had expanded. I wanted to help others conquer addiction. Though I realized that, until I had more sobriety, I wasn't in a position to coach anyone else. I talked to groups about being an addict, but I was careful to focus on my recovery now, versus acting like I had it licked.

You never have it licked, after all. The experts say the first year is the most difficult. They say if you make it through your first year, you have a 90 percent chance of staying sober the rest of your life.

My six-month anniversary of sobriety—August 12, 1997—was a big deal to me.

Each month after that I said to Mary, "Well, Mur"—that's my nickname for her—"today's seven months," or whatever it was. She'd congratulate me and give me a hug. When it was eleven months, I got scared. Especially the last ten days, the last week. A year of sobriety! I was anxious.

I woke up about a quarter after midnight Thursday, February 12, 1998, so excited. "Mur!" I whispered. "It's been a year!" She rolled over and gave me a hug and a kiss. I was really excited. It was like being little. I felt like it was my birthday and I had a big party to look forward to.

You talk to people who've been in recovery for a while, and sometimes they can say, "It's been eleven years, 310 days." I'm not like that, but I was very proud to have that first year behind me. That morning when I started my on-air shift at the radio station, I said, "Folks, I just want to say something here. It's not to pat myself on the back, but it's to let you know that you *can* get a grip on a terrible disease. You all know about my addiction. Today's my one-year anniversary of sobriety. I couldn't have done it without a lot of help from a lot of people. If anyone listening wants to talk to me, just call. Enough said. But I did want to say thank you to everyone who's helped."

Right away one of the businesses in town faxed me a nice note, and everyone I bumped into that day congratulated me. Other people wrote letters. It was clear I'd touched people already, just in my first year.

Now I'm racking up *years* of sobriety, and it feels great.

I reflect a lot on why I've stayed sober. For one thing, I did what I was told. I followed the twelve-step program, I listened to my counselors, and I went to all the meetings.

For another, I believed I could do it.

The biggest reason I got better, I think, is that I *really wanted to*. I finally reached a point where I knew if I didn't get help, I would die.

I think some people who continually get arrested for drunken driving or whatever it is don't necessarily want to get better. It seems that way at least. For now they're not interested in giving up alcohol, they like it that much. I can relate. If I would have gotten caught forging prescriptions a month or two earlier than I did, I wouldn't necessarily have been ready to sober up.

It was just in the week before I got caught that I really had any serious interest in getting help. I was running out of excuses to give Mary, I was running out of money to buy drugs, and rather than a feeling of euphoria, they were making me sick.

I hit the proverbial bottom just in time.

People say, "Dick, is recovering from drug addiction as hard as running marathons?" And I say, "Man, it's not even close. It's not even close."

It isn't. Training for a marathon or running a marathon is such a walk to the mailbox compared to beating an addiction. It's the hardest thing I've ever been through, emotionally or physically.

The withdrawal from methadone was a physical challenge

I hope I'm never faced with again. Even years later, it sounds more fun to peel my skin back and soak what's left in rubbing alcohol.

But it's one of the best things that ever happened to me.

Because for one thing, I'm no longer afraid of death. I'm more sure than ever that God has a mission for me, and he'll keep me safe until that's complete. For now I know it's my job to speak to others about this disease, and offer them hope that it's something you can beat if you want to badly enough. I've always been a yakker, and this just gives me something else to relate to people about—something important.

That's why I like working in radio. I practice my speaking. Mostly I talk about the weather, or what song's coming up. But I can picture the people who might be listening. I can slip in a story once in a while and imagine folks in town chuckling. Sometimes I'll look out the window and see a little gopher running around and pretend the gopher's a hundred people out there listening to me talk.

To me there's no feeling like telling a story about my addiction or how I keep myself motivated and having people on the edge of their seats—like they can't wait to hear what's next. Having that connection with an audience is better than any drug. I honestly think I live to inspire people.

Out of five hundred people listening to a talk, maybe one person will remember something I said enough to take it to heart and change their life. That's what I live for. And it was worth all the hell I went through.

I wouldn't wish all this pain on Mary and Andy, but if they can forgive me, it has been for the best.

I mean that. I am the *luckiest man alive.*

Life has never been this sweet.

Mary's busy managing the Best Western Holland House and Suites in Detroit Lakes, where we live. Andy's in high school and doing really well.

Life has never been this *normal.* What I consider normal,

anyway. I get up every morning at three-thirty and go for a five-mile run. I'm at the radio station until about noon, then work as a fishing guide the rest of the day.

There aren't a lot of guys I know who make their living as a fishing guide. I mean, really, how many people are you acquainted with who really, *really* love their work? I do. Dad was right, I'll never get wealthy doing it. But wealth is overrated. You can have your stock options and all the headaches it took to get them. I'll just grab a ham sandwich and head back out on the boat.

As for running, I enjoy it more now than I ever have. So many friends warned me I wouldn't, once I quit running 2:10 marathons. They couldn't have been more wrong. Since my very first run, I've loved what it does for me, mentally and physically. I've always run as much for my head as anything else, and now it's a critical part of my sobriety. Forty-five minutes of reflection out there on the road every morning is enough to stay in shape and keep the stress at bay.

I *love* running. It's still my favorite thing to do.

It's even more precious to me now because of how many times it was almost taken away from me. Of course, no one loves it more than my dog, Coal. Once in a while it's kind of hard for me to get out of bed at three-thirty in the morning, but not for him. He loves it. The colder the better, too.

It's hard for me to believe, but my 2:08:53 at Boston is still the fourth-fastest marathon time by an American runner. Salazar's time is number three. Another Minnesota boy is the second fastest. Bob Kempainen finished in seventh place at the 1994 Boston, but clocked a 2:08:47. Khalid Khannouchi of New York ranks number one. He ran a 2:07:01 in Chicago in October 2000.

In September I run the Dick Beardsley Half Marathon here. This year will be the seventh annual.

I don't run marathons anymore, but I made an exception

for the twenty-fifth anniversary of Grandma's. I finished in 2:55:39, which tickled me.

Every day I start over in the toughest race, though: staying sober.

No matter how many years of sobriety I rack up, I'll always identify with the person just starting out. Because we're all in the same boat. It's day to day, the struggle. You can never take it for granted, no matter how long you've been sober. Every day's your first day.

Suppose I'm out running and find a bottle of Percocet in the ditch. Would I take it? Or would I throw it in the lake? What would I do?

A few years ago, I don't know.

I think now I would throw it in the lake.

DICK BEARDSLEY is a former world-class distance runner who holds the fourth-fastest marathon time by an American male. His first-place finish at Duluth's Grandma's Marathon in 1981 remains a course record; he also holds the course record for the Napa Valley Marathon, set in 1987. In 1982 he won the Robert E. DeCelle Award, which recognizes the outstanding U.S. male distance runner, and in 1990 he was named Comeback Runner of the Year by *Runner's World* magazine. He is a member of the Road Runners Club of America Hall of Fame and is listed in the *Guinness Book of World Records* for the longest consecutive string of faster marathon times (thirteen).

He has been a fishing guide for thirty years and is also a professional public speaker.

MAUREEN ANDERSON is a freelance writer and award-winning radio journalist. Her syndicated radio program *The Career Clinic* is broadcast worldwide.

Both authors are eager to hear from you. You can reach either of them by e-mail at feedback@stayingthecourse.com.